# *Eminent Domain*

## A PLAY

### *by Percy Granger*

SAMUEL FRENCH, INC.

25 West 45th Street      NEW YORK 10036

7623 Sunset Boulevard      HOLLYWOOD 90046

*LONDON*      *TORONTO*

EMINENT DOMAIN was first presented in a staged reading at the Eugene O'Neill's National Playwrights' Conference in 1977. It was subsequently given a workshop production at the Seattle Repertory's Second Stage in 1978.

The first full production was by the Peterborough Players in August, 1979, with the following cast:

| | |
|---|---|
| Holmes Bradford | Jess Adkins |
| Katie Bradford | Rosanna Cox |
| Victor Salt | Richmond Hoxie |
| Stoddard Oates | Jonathan Niles |
| John Ramsey | Eric Conger |

It was directed by Charles Morey.

In January, 1981, it opened at the McCarter Theatre in Princeton, New Jersey, with the following cast:

| | |
|---|---|
| Holmes Bradford | MacIntyre Dixon |
| Katie Bradford | Betty Miller |
| Victor Salt | Stephen Stout |
| Stoddard Oates | Thomas Nahrwold |
| John Ramsey | Barry Boys |

It was directed by Paul Austin.

It opened on Broadway at Circle-in-the-Square on March 28, 1982, with the following cast:

| | |
|---|---|
| Holmes Bradford | Philip Bosco |
| Katie Bradford | Betty Miller |
| Victor Salt | John Vickery |
| Stoddard Oates | Scott Burkholder |
| John Ramsey | Paul Collins |

It was directed by Paul Austin.

Time
February, 1975
Place
A university town in the midwest
*THERE WILL BE ONE INTERMISSION*

Opening Night March 28, 1982

# CIRCLE IN THE SQUARE

**Theodore Mann**
Artistic Director

**Paul Libin**
Managing Director

presents

# PHILIP BOSCO
# BETTY MILLER

in

# eminent
# domain

a new play by

# PERCY GRANGER

with

**SCOTT
BURKHOLDER**

**PAUL
COLLINS**

and

# JOHN VICKERY

Scenery by
**MICHAEL
MILLER**

Costumes by
**JENNIFER
VON MAYRHAUSER**

Lighting by
**LOWELL
ACHZIGER**

Directed by

# PAUL AUSTIN

"Eminent Domain" was first presented as a staged reading at the National Playwrights Conference of the Eugene O'Neill Centre and further developed in productions at the Peterborough Players in New Hampshire and the McCarter Theatre in Princeton.

The Producers and the Theatre Management of the Circle in the Square are members of the League of New York Theatres and Producers, Inc.

EMINENT DOMAIN, descriptive story:

EMINENT DOMAIN is about a worthy but eccentric professor and his wife, once a painter of great promise, now a reformed alcoholic who has retreated into a hermetic existence. The story deals with their crisis as they approach old age. For years his career has been at a standstill and now he has a final chance to escape his midwestern cow college and assume a prestigious Chair back east. But his insistence upon the illusion that he and his wife can thereby regain the lost days of their youth, and that everything will be better once she returns to her painting, threaten to dissolve the marriage. Further pressure is brought to bear by the arrival of a brilliantly promising graduate student from Harvard who is writing a thesis on their son, an emerging poet who left home abruptly eight years before and has not been in touch since. The thesis, we learn, will also be published as a book and the author needs biographical information. The professor feels an obligation to help; his wife, embarrassed by her failures and struggling to maintain a hard won inner peace, is determined that her life is no one's business but her own.

One set.

Five characters: four male, one female

## CAST

HOLMES BRADFORD
KATIE BRADFORD
VICTOR SALT
STODDARD OATES
JOHN RAMSEY

## SETTING

A university town in the southern midwest.
February, 1975.

## SYNOPSIS OF SCENES

Scene 1: Late Tuesday night
Scene 2: Wednesday morning
Scene 3: Thursday afternoon
Scene 4: Thursday night
Scene 5: Friday morning
Scene 6: Friday afternoon

The suggested act break is after Scene Two. It may, however, come after Scene Three.

## THE SET

The BRADFORD house.

Two rooms are visible, the living room and the study. Upstage of the living room through an archway the foyer is also visible. The front door is s.r. and the first half-dozen steps of a stairway are visible leading up and off towards s.l. Beside the stairway is a hallway exit.

The two rooms are in sharp contrast. The living room is painted white and sparsely furnished. There is a handsome round wooden table and chair in the center of the room. Along the imaginary wall between the two rooms is a Windsor settee, attractive to the eye but uninviting to the would-be lounger. A side table with extra shelves along the wall u.r.c. by the study door is the room's only other furniture. There is a built-in window seat beneath the window s.r. Beside this, wastebasket. The window has curtains which remain drawn back until the play's final scene. About the room are three or four urns and vases filled with arrangements of dried grasses, leaves and weeds. A simple chandelier hangs over the round table; its light switch is on the wall by the archway. There are no rugs on the polished wooden floor.

The study by contrast is dark and jammed. The grey-green walls are mostly masked with floor to ceiling bookcases which sag under the weight of books crammed in every which way. There is a functional door to the living room, a closet on the back wall, and a window obscured by heavy dark-colored drapes over the wooden desk. In addition to the desk, the furnishings include an old wooden knock-about chair, a standing file cabinet with four drawers, a swivel chair, an overstuffed reading chair, a small side table, a standing lamp, and an army cot. With the exception of the cot all the furniture is old and worn. There are several layers of Persian rugs on the floor. The desk and file cabinet are piled high with books, magazines, journals, papers, blue books, etc. There are numerous calendars and lists taped to the side of the cabinet; there is a phone on the desk, and a drowned potted plant atop the file cabinet.

Behind the set two files depict the outside upper story of the house, a white-washed, wood-frame structure with a steep-pitched roof; in feeling, a classic midwestern farmhouse.

# Eminent Domain

*The standing lamp in the study fades up, revealling* HOLMES *asleep in his reading chair, his head resting on a pillow, an open book propped up against his chest. When groomed* HE *is an attractive vigorous man in his early sixties. But at the moment his hair is rumpled and exhaustion shows in his face.* HE *wears a thermal-knit nightshift and an old loosely-tied flannel robe. The study door is closed.*

*After a few moments the overhead light comes up in the living room to reveal* KATIE, *seated at her table, working meticulously doing calligraphic lettering with pen and ink on a poster.* SHE *is an attractive quiet woman in her late fifties.* SHE *wears a flannel nightgown and a corduroy housecoat.*

SHE *dips her pen into the inkwell, draws off the excess ink on a pad, and letters. The third time* SHE *does this her hand trembles.* SHE *grabs it with her other hand until the trembling passes, then wipes her pen clean and rises to retire.*

HOLMES *snores.* KATIE *looks up, glances at her watch, then goes to the study door and knocks lightly.*

KATIE. Holmes? (*No response.* SHE *enters quietly.* HOLMES *opens his eyes.*)

11

HOLMES. Katie, that you?

KATIE. Yes.

HOLMES. Was I asleep?

KATIE. (*Pouring the last of the water from the pitcher on a tray near the door into a glass.*) Your face was relaxed.

HOLMES. (*Rubbing his eyes.*) Uh.

KATIE. It's almost time for bed. Here. (SHE *hands him the glass, and kisses him lightly on the top of his head.*) Good night, dear. Sleep well. (SHE *exits with the water tray.* HOLMES *stares at the water and grunts;* HE *turns the alarm clock on his desk to see the time.*)

HOLMES. Fifteen more minutes . . . (HE *takes a sip of water, makes a face and pours the rest into the potted plant.* HE *rises stiffly, sets the glass back on the tray, and looks out the door to make sure* KATIE *is gone.* HE *closes the door quietly and reaches out a bottle of bourbon and a glass from behind a row of books.* HE *pours himself a shot, drinks; pours another, drinks that, then turns to the calendar taped on the side of the file cabinet.*) What've we got, the nineteenth? (HE *checks a list beside the calendar.*) . . . Edward Taylor. (HE *opens the file cabinet and takes out a folder of yellowed lecture notes.* HE *opens it and regards them.*) "In what way does the poetry of Edward Taylor reflect the unrefined lumpishness of an embryonic frontier society?" (*Pause.* HE *glances about as if at an unresponsive class.*) "In what way does the poetry of Edward Taylor reflect the statement, 'American poetry is a series of new beginnings'?" (*Pause.*) In what way does the poetry of Edward Taylor reflect the preparation you have done for this class? (*Pause.* HE *pours another drink, muttering:*) Basset hounds. (HE *drinks, and checks the alarm clock.*) Thirteen more minutes. (HE *puts the folder in*

*the briefcase and scans a bookshelf for the appropriate
volume to accompany them.*) (*There is a KNOCK at the
front door.*) (HOLMES *starts and quickly hides the bottle
and glass behind a stack of magazines on the desk.*) (*Irritably.*) Katie? (*No response.* HE *pops a mint into his
mouth and carefully opens the study door and looks
out. Again, the KNOCK.* HOLMES *goes to the front
door, spitting the mint into the wastebasket on the way.*
HE *tightens the belt on his robe.* HE *opens the door. A*
YOUNG MAN, *sharply dressed in trenchcoat and a grey
wool suit, stands smiling at him.*)
(*Curtly.*) Yes?

    VICTOR. Dr. Bradford, I presume?

    HOLMES. Yes?

    VICTOR. (*Gives a small, smart salute.*) Salt here.

    HOLMES. What?

    VICTOR. I'm Victor Salt. (*A beat.*) From Harvard.

    HOLMES. (*Remembering.*) Oh yes.

    VICTOR. I know it's late —

    HOLMES. Come in, come in. It's colder than a brass
monkey's balls out there.

    VICTOR. Thank you. (HE *steps in;* HOLMES *shuts the
door.*)

    HOLMES. I wasn't expecting you till tomorrow was I?

    VICTOR. No. I was going to go straight to a motel,
but —

    HOLMES. Good lord. This hasn't been Wednesday has
it?

    VICTOR. No, I —

    HOLMES. Thank god. For a moment I was afraid I'd
given the same lecture twice.

    VICTOR. I saw your light on.

    HOLMES. Well then there's still hope.

    VICTOR. I mean that's why I stopped.

HOLMES. (*Patiently.*) I know. (*Gesturing towards the study.*) Go in there, Mrs. Bradford's deviled with insomnia.

VICTOR. Oh. I'm sorry.

HOLMES. So am I. (HE *follows* VICTOR *in and shuts the door.*)

VICTOR. (*Taking in the room.*) Wow.

HOLMES. What?

VICTOR. This room.

HOLMES. Uh. It must go down nine layers by now like the ruins of ancient Troy. If we ever moved we'd have to hire archaeologists instead of Mayflower. (HE *notices water dripping from the plant down the file cabinet. HE mops it up with a corner of his robe.*)

VICTOR. I've looked forward to meeting you for so long I can't believe I'm finally here.

HOLMES. Take off your coat. You look like a manikin.

VICTOR. Oh sorry. (HE *undoes his coat.* HOLMES *goes down on his knees to mop up the water on the rug.*)

HOLMES. How was your trip?

VICTOR. I drove straight through.

HOLMES. What, all the way from Cambridge?

VICTOR. (*Rubbing his hands together vigorously.*) Yes sir.

HOLMES. What's the rush, we aren't going anywhere.

VICTOR. I find travel a waste of time.

HOLMES. (*Giving him the once-over.*) Huh. Yes, I've heard you're quite the young turk at Harvard.

VICTOR. Thank you.

HOLMES. Do you sit?

VICTOR. No. I mean no, I won't stay. I know it's late.

HOLMES. Oh sit down, I never go to bed before twelve. I've still got ten minutes.

VICTOR. Okay. Thanks. (HE *sits.*) I trust my dissertation arrived safely?

HOLMES. Oh yes. (VICTOR *sits forward expectantly, but* HOLMES *turns and, during the following speech, finds the book he was looking for and puts it in his briefcase.*) I went to Harvard myself you know. Your dissertation director, Jerry MacKay, and I were graduate students together. He got an appointment; I didn't. I was slow out of the gate, as they say.

VICTOR. You've certainly made up for lost time.

HOLMES. No one makes up for lost time, Victor.

VICTOR. Dr. MacKay says you're being offered a post at Brandeis.

HOLMES. Yes. It's a Chair actually. It's not Harvard, but at least it will get Katie and me back east for our twilight years and that's what we've always wanted. You must be sober after driving all that way. You want a drink?

VICTOR. Oh—no thanks. I don't drink.

HOLMES. (*Stopped in the act of getting a glass from behind the books.*) Eh?

VICTOR. I don't drink.

HOLMES. I don't understand. Are you sure?

VICTOR. Quite. I'm conserving my brain cells.

HOLMES. Oh. (*As* HE *pours himself a final libation:*) Perhaps you'd rather not watch then. I squander mine at an alarming rate. I wade in and hack away like Attila the Hun.

VICTOR. Have you had a chance to read it?

HOLMES. You hungry?

VICTOR. Wha—oh, no. thanks.

HOLMES. Would you like something non-alcoholic, like a beer?

VICTOR. No.

HOLMES. Do you want to use the bathroom?

VICTOR. I took care of that already.

HOLMES. No basic needs, eh? That's an enviable condition. At least loosen your tie, unless it's holding your head on.

VICTOR. (*Rising; tight-lipped.*) I'm sorry.

HOLMES. What?

VICTOR. I shouldn't have stopped so late.

HOLMES. (*Surprised.*) Did I offend you?

VICTOR. I'll call you in the morning.

HOLMES. From where?

VICTOR. I'll find a motel.

HOLMES. Why don't you stay with us?

VICTOR. Oh —

HOLMES. You've driven all this way, it's the least we can do. We can start over again in the morning.

VICTOR. Well — thanks. I'd be honored.

HOLMES. Good.

VICTOR. Would that be all right with Mrs. Bradford?

HOLMES. It'll be good for her, give her something to do.

VICTOR. Well — fine. Thank you. Where do I go?

HOLMES. Right here. (HE *indicates the cot.*)

VICTOR. In here?

HOLMES. It's the only spare rack in the house. (*Unfolding the blanket and spreading it over the cot.*) Katie uses Wendel's old room, and the second floor isn't furnished except for my room. Here, I've even got a pillow. (HE *gets the pillow from his reading chair.*) There. Oh — do you need sheets?

VICTOR. (*Yes.*) No. No, this is fine. Thank you.

HOLMES. (*As* HE *puts the glasses and bourbon away.*) Stout lad. Between my hooch and that cot this room's equipped to withstand a seige of up to three months, a prospect that becomes more attractive with every passing day . . . You got luggage?

VICTOR. Oh — yes.

HOLMES. Get it. I lock up before going to bed. The

nights here are filled with savage athletes on full scholarship. (*As soon as* VICTOR *is gone* HOLMES *turns and mutters:*) Mother of god . . .

(HE *scrambles about the study looking high and low until* HE *finds the object of his search,* VICTOR'S *dissertation. It is under a pile of stuff on the file cabinet. Its mailing envelope is stuck in the first few pages as a book-mark.* HE *hears* VICTOR *re-enter and quickly crumples the envelope and throws it away and displays the dissertation prominently on his desk.* VICTOR *locks the door and hangs his trench coat on the coat tree and re-enters the study with a suitcase and attache case. Both expensive; both new.* HOLMES *straightens up quickly with a smile.*)

VICTOR. I locked the door for you.

HOLMES. Thanks. (*The alarm clock RINGS.* VICTOR *starts.*) Hup, that's my cue. (HE *shuts it off.*) I'm a pumpkin.

VICTOR. Are you sure this is all right?

HOLMES. (*As* HE *pockets the clock and picks up his briefcase.*) I have to be up at cockcrow but you feel free to sleep in.

VICTOR. I don't use much sleep.

HOLMES. Nonsense, you must be exhausted. I'll leave a note for Katie to alert her you're here. (HE *puts a hand on* VICTOR'S *shoulder.*) It'll be nice to have some young blood in the house again. Keep us on our toes. Good night, son.

(HE *goes.* HE *sets his briefcase by the foot of the stairs, turns out the overhead light in the living room, unlocks and locks the front door, and disappears up the stairs.* VICTOR *meanwhile undresses as* HE *scrutinizes the study.* HE *sees the dissertation on the desk and leafs through it to see if there are any marginal comments. There are none, nor is the cover creased as it would be if it had been read.* HE *frowns slightly and glances towards the closed study door as:*)

## LIGHTS FADE TO BLACK

### SCENE TWO

*The following morning.*

*Bright morning light streams in through the living room window.* VICTOR, *in his underwear is sound asleep under the blanket.* KATIE, *in her nightgown and housecoat, enters the living room by the downstairs hallway with a cup of coffee on a saucer and crosses to her table.* SHE *regards the poster on which* SHE *has evidently once again been working.* SHE *picks up a pen to correct some minor fault, stops herself from fussing, starts again, stops, and finally unable to resist the perfectionist's impulse,* SHE *dips the pen in the ink, draws off the excess, and makes a small adjustment. Then* SHE *glances at her watch, goes to the front door, opens it and takes the mail from the mailbox.* SHE *drifts back into the living room sorting her mail from* HOLMES'. SHE *puts hers on her table, then enters the study.* SHE *checks a thermometer by the door, turns on the space heater, and is about to put* HOLMES' *mail on the desk when* SHE *sees* VICTOR. SHE *starts, then moves closer to try to get a look at his face.* VICTOR *wakens with a start and sits up.* KATIE *steps back quickly.*

VICTOR. I'm from Harvard!

KATIE. Excuse me—

VICTOR. (*Looks at his watch.*) Oh Jesus I never sleep this late, really.

KATIE. Who are you?

VICTOR. Victor.

KATIE. . . . Was Holmes expecting you?

VICTOR. He said he'd leave a note warning you I was here.

KATIE. Oh.

VICTOR. Golly, I hope he wasn't angry. I arrived late last night as he was on his way to bed.

KATIE. (*Recovered from her initial shock,* SHE *smiles tentatively.*) Holmes is a man of strict regimen. You mustn't take it personally.

VICTOR. You're Mrs. Bradford?

KATIE. Yes, I'm sorry.

VICTOR. (*Smiles as* HE *wraps the blanket around him and puts his feet on the floor.*) The power behind the throne.

KATIE. What?

VICTOR. I'm the fellow doing his doctoral dissertation on your son, on his poetry.

KATIE. . . . Would you like some lunch?

VICTOR. Lunch? Really, I never sleep this late.

KATIE. Breakfast?

VICTOR. Coffee would be welcome if it's no trouble.

KATIE. Not at all. Mornings are my best time.

(SHE *exits, pulling the door to behind her, drops* HOLMES' *mail on the side table, and disappears towards the kitchen.* VICTOR *rises quickly, pulls on a pair of slacks from his suitcase, slips into his shoes, picks up his shaving kit and a shirt from the suitcase, does one quick energetic toe-touch, and goes into the living room. Realizing* HE *has no idea where the bathroom is,* HE *stops.* HE *turns to take in the living room, then sets his shaving kit down for a closer look.* HE *studies the poster on the table, glances out the window — and then is stopped cold by something on the fourth wall — a painting.* HE *moves in and bends to read the signature, then backs up slowly, regarding it with growing interest.* KATIE *reappears with a cup and saucer.* SHE *registers his absorbtion, then breaks into it.*)

KATIE. I took the liberty of adding milk to give you some sustenance.

VICTOR. (*Charmed by her liberty.*) Oh, thanks.

KATIE. I'm sorry Holmes isn't back yet. They have their Departmental meetings on Wednesdays.

VICTOR. Please don't let me distrub you.

KATIE. (*Busying herself cleaning her pens.*) Oh no, I'm finished for the day.

VICTOR. (*Looking over her shoulder.*) Chancery cursive isn't it?

KATIE. Yes.

VICTOR. I know something about calligraphy.

KATIE. It's just a poster for our local arts and crafts place. We're having a medieval fair this spring.

VICTOR. You have an artistic flare. A nice way with coffee too.

KATIE. It's the one thing I make from scratch.

VICTOR. (*Turning again to the painting.*) This is a most interesting painting . . . Marvellous actually. (*Looking at the signature.*) "Ingraham" . . . I know that name . . . (*He frowns, trying to remember.*)

KATIE. (*Taking the tray of pens and inks to her side tabe.*) You're writing a whole dissertation about Wendel?

VICTOR. I maintain he's our first significant new voice in twenty years.

KATIE. Really?

VICTOR. I believe I make a pretty good case for it. You know of course he's got a good shot at the Pulitzer this year.

KATIE. Oh.

VICTOR. (HE *frowns.*) . . . Dr. Bradford hasn't mentioned me at all?

KATIE. I'm sure he did and I forgot. I'm sorry. If you'd like to wash up, the bathroom is down the hall on your left.

VICTOR. Yes, of course, Excuse me.

(VICTOR, *feeling very awkward, sets his cup and saucer on the round table and crosses for his shaving kit. As* HE *starts off:*)

KATIE. How did you know Wendel was our son?

VICTOR. My dissertation director knew Dr. Bradford at Harvard. He made the connection.

KATIE. Do you know where he is?

VICTOR. No.

KATIE. Did he ask you not to tell us?

VICTOR. I've never met him, Mrs. Bradford. I don't think anyone knows where he is, not even his publishers.

KATIE. Of course. I'm sorry, I didn't mean to stop you.

VICTOR. (*After a hesitation* HE *ventures:*) It's been eight years since he left?

KATIE. Yes.

VICTOR. And Dr. Bradford said you haven't heard from him in all that time?

KATIE. If privacy is what he wants I can understand that.

VICTOR. Why?

KATIE. Why not?

VICTOR. (*Smiles.*) Touché. Well, I hope we'll have a chance to talk further.

KATIE. (*Putting her lettering books away in the window seat.*) Oh I'm afraid I don't know much about poetry.

VICTOR. I mean about you.

KATIE. Me?

VICTOR. My editor's asked me to generate profiles on you and Dr. Bradford.

KATIE. Editor? You said this was a dissertation.

VICTOR. It is, but it's going to be published.

KATIE. In a journal?

VICTOR. As a book. I've timed it quite well. As you can imagine, people are becoming very curious about Wendel and his background. The publishers think an opening biographical chapter will further our understanding of the poetry.

KATIE. (*Small smile.*) Oh, dear, I hope you don't expect us to be colorful.

VICTOR. Whatever. Is there someplace I can set up shop? Some corner where I wouldn't be in the way?

KATIE. There's nothing, really.

VICTOR. One of the rooms upstairs?

KATIE. That's not furnished except for Holmes room.

VICTOR. Oh?

KATIE. There's only my old studio in the attic.

VICTOR. Studio?

KATIE. But it hasn't been used in years. It's not even heated.

VICTOR. I can work anywhere. I've got the blood of a fish. You *are* an artist then.

KATIE. It was just something I used to do. (VICTOR *makes the connection with the painting.*)

VICTOR. "*K*. Ingraham"—Katie? Is this yours?

KATIE. That was my maiden name.

VICTOR. Really? (HE *regards the painting with renewed interest*.) Well this *is* interesting . . . I know something about art; my father has a gallery in Boston.

KATIE. I only painted because it didn't involve lifting anything heavy or dealing with people.

VICTOR. You stopped?

KATIE. Years ago.

VICTOR. Why?

KATIE. It's not something I need to do any more.

VICTOR. That's too bad.

KATIE. Not really. I do some teaching now.

VICTOR. Are there more canvases upstirs?

KATIE. Yes, but—

VICTOR. Ingraham! Are you related to Magda Ingraham, the woman who founded the Pembroke Colony in Maine?

KATIE. She was my mother.

VICTOR. Really? But my father knew her, he exhibited her. You're her daughter? He'd love to meet you when you come back East.

KATIE. East?

VICTOR. Next fall, when Dr. Bradford takes the Brandeis Chair.

KATIE. What?

VICTOR. The Chair they're endowing in American Poetry.

KATIE. Does Holmes know about this?

VICTOR. Yes. Don't you?

KATIE. No.

VICTOR. Oh. Oh dear, maybe he meant it as a surprise.

KATIE. It is.

VICTOR. (*Anxiously*.) Please don't tell him I spoiled it until he tells me what he thinks of my dissertation.

(*Awkwardly.*) Maybe I should just go and get my act together before he returns. Excuse me.

(HE *exits towards the bathroom.* KATIE *goes to the window to look for a sign of* HOLMES; SHE *evidently sees him and sits on the window box facing the front door to wait. In a moment* HOLMES *enters with his briefcase.* HE *wears an old over coat, a tweed jacket, colored woolen shirt with bow or straight tie, and a hat. There is a white piece of paper scotch-taped to one lens of his glasses.* HE *is harassed and out of sorts.*)

HOLMES. (*Calling down the hallway.*) Katie? Are you up? (*Without waiting for an answer* HE *crosses to her table and removes a manila folder from his briefcase.*)

KATIE. (*Rising.*) Holmes —

HOLMES. Oh. Here's the list of the new Phi Beta Kappa members. I've written out the letter, all you have to do is type copies. The usual thing. (HE *drops the folder carelessly on her poster.*)

KATIE. Be careful, this isn't dry. (SHE *picks the folder up quickly and checks the poster.* HOLMES *ignores this and brushes past her into the study.* KATIE *gets some correction fluid from her side table and carefully whites out a smudge on the poster during the following.*)

HOLMES. I've lost one of these god-damned lenses again, you'll have to fish it out for me. (HE *searches his desk.*) No mail?

KATIE. What?

HOLMES. (*Irritably.*) Mail. Mail.

KATIE. Yes.

HOLMES. But none for me? . . . Katie?

KATIE. It's out here. (HOLMES *returns to the living room. As* HE *takes it,* SHE *puts the cap back on the fluid.*) I was pushed a bit off stride today. (HOLMES *seems not to hear this,* HE *strides to the window and glances out as* HE *sorts through his mail.*) Holmes —

HOLMES. Well the fat's in the fire now. We voted this morning to deny tenure to John Ramsey, and there will no doubt be a howl of protest. But we've handled the babes in arms before. (HE *glances at her.*) No need to look so concerned, hon. (HE *indicates the poster.*) I'm sorry, is that okay?

KATIE. What's this about a Chair?

HOLMES. What? What chair?

KATIE. At Brandeis.

HOLMES. Where'd you hear about that?

KATIE. From a young man I found sleeping on your cot.

HOLMES. Oh good lord, I'd forgotten all about him. Where is he?

KATIE. In the bathroom, getting his act together.

HOLMES. You met him then.

KATIE. Why didn't you tell me he was here?

HOLMES. (*Slight edge.*) Because you were still asleep when I left this morning.

KATIE. Did you invite him to stay here?

HOLMES. You can handle that, can't you?

KATIE. Do you want him sleeping in your study?

HOLMES. Not especially. Would you like to propose the logistical alternative?

KATIE. Why, couldn't he stay in a motel?

HOLMES. No. I'm not making an issue out of it, am I, but the boy stays here, and I don't want him to see us fussing like a couple of children. (HE *tosses most of his mail, unopened, in the wastebasket, and crosses past her into the study.*)

KATIE. And this Chair? How long have you known about that?

HOLMES. It's not definite yet. I've been approached but their Trustees still have to approve my selection.

KATIE. When do you hear?

HOLMES. Friday.

KATIE. This Friday?

HOLMES. (*Avoiding her gaze; taking letterhead stationary from his file cabinet.*) Yes this Friday.

KATIE. Why on earth didn't you tell me? What could you have been thinking of?

HOLMES. (*Gruffly.*) I didn't want you fretting till I knew for certain. It won't be till next fall anyway, there's plenty of time to get used to the idea. (*An edge of contrition creeps into his voice.*) You feel up to it now don't you, a move?

KATIE. Well I don't know, it's all so sudden.

HOLMES. It's time, you know it is.

KATIE. Yes, but—

HOLMES. What a finale, eh? To assume a Chair in American Poetry? The triumphant return of the exiles from the heartland?

KATIE. It's bad luck to want something too much.

HOLMES. (*With playful mock caution.*) Of course it is. But let us break with tradition and once again hope for the best. Shhh. (HE *hands her the stationery.*) Here's for the Phi Beta letters. How're your hands today?

KATIE. I don't know, they began trembling earlier when I was working.

HOLMES. (*Indicating his eye.*) You think you can get this thing out?

KATIE. I can try. Come into the light. (SHE *puts the stationary on the side table;* HOLMES *follows her out, but pauses to cast an anxious glance in the direction of the bathroom.* KATIE *rubs her hands.*)

HOLMES. What do you make of our visitor. Did you take his measure?

KATIE. He seems very ambitious.

HOLMES. Well I've seen his kind before.

KATIE. What kind?

HOLMES. Young.

KATIE. Sit. (HOLMES *sits on the window seat.*)

HOLMES. World beaters out to make a name for themselves.

KATIE. He says his dissertation is going to be published.

HOLMES. Really. Good for him, I haven't published anything in five years . . .

KATIE. (*Tilting his head back.*) Hold still.

HOLMES. He'll be a good tune-up for Brandeis, um?

KATIE. Shh. (SHE *makes a tenative dab at his eye.*)

HOLMES. Ow. Think 'steady'.

KATIE. (*Small smile.*) That just makes it worse.

HOLMES. Will power.

KATIE. Sh. Hold still. (VICTOR *enters, groomed.*)

VICTOR. Good morning, sir.

HOLMES. (*Looking over.*) Eh? Ow! (*To* KATIE.) All right, all right, let it be. (HE *rises and dons his most affable social manner despite his pain.*) Good morning, Victor. (HE *offers his hand;* THEY *shake.*) I gather you met my wife? Katie—Victor Salt.

VICTOR. Indeed.

HOLMES. You see before you a rare and extraordinary woman, Victor. She's an *artiste* too, like our absent son, though she probably didn't tell you. I'm the only drudge in the family. Say, how are you with contacts?

VICTOR. I know something about them.

HOLMES. See if you can fetch this one out of my eye . . . see it?

VICTOR. Yep . . . Got it.

HOLMES. Deftly done.

VICTOR. Have you got a lens case?

HOLMES. (*Patting himself down.*) Somewhere. I had my second cataract operation over Christmas break and I still can't cope with these damn things. I've torn two and lost one. I'm too incompetent to be old. Damn, it's fallen into the lining again. Front and center, to the rear. (HE *draws himself to attention and does an about face.* KATIE *works the case around back to the hole in the pocket.*) "Ma and Pa Kettle grind to a halt." Don't be alarmed, Victor, Katie frequently milks me before lunch.

KATIE. Have you got your spares?

HOLMES. (*To* VICTOR.) Yes. Fetch my briefcase would you?

VICTOR. Yes, sir. (VICTOR *goes into the study and* KATIE *keeps working.*)

HOLMES. (*Under his breath.*) I thought you were going to mend this for me.

KATIE. There are three perfectly good suits hanging in your closet. There. (VICTOR *returns with briefcase as* KATIE *finds the lens case.*)

HOLMES. (*Resuming his sociable tone.*) Good.

KATIE. Give it to me, I have to clean it. (VICTOR *hands her the lens.* HOLMES *takes the briefcase and heads for the study.*)

HOLMES. Come on in, Victor. Coffee, Katie? (KATIE *turns to respond but* HOLMES *is already through the door.* SHE *goes.* HOLMES *eases himself into the chair at his desk.*) Thank god, I never thought I'd make it. Another day when I might just as well have measured out my life in coffee spoons. (HOLMES *takes his extra lenses from his briefcase and puts in the needed one.* VICTOR *sits on the cot and prepares for their expected talk by taking a second copy of the dissertation from his attache case; also a pen, note-pad, and tape recorder. As* HE *does so,* HE *talks.*)

VICTOR. I've been on tenterhooks for days. I wanted to call before I left Cambridge but I didn't dare. I feel like a kid. (HOLMES *has successfully inserted the lens.* HE *blinks and grins.*)

HOLMES. Ah. But it's the minor triumphs that keep us going isn't it. (HE *rises.*)

VICTOR. So. What do you think?

HOLMES. (*Closing the door.*) I think we should have a drink.

VICTOR. Drink?

HOLMES. The only civilized way to kick off a working relationship, don't you agree? (HOLMES *turns to the bookcase to fetch out two glasses and the bourbon bottle.* VICTOR *glances at his watch.*) I have to keep it behind the Trancendentalists here. Mrs. Bradford mustn't know I use my inner sanctum for fantastical interluding. She's a teetotaler now, though she used to like her nip. I trust my secret is safe with you?

VICTOR. Absolutely. But I —

HOLMES. There you go.

VICTOR. (*Taking the proffered glass.*) Thanks.

HOLMES. (*Raising his glass.*) May you die with the teeth you were born with. (HE *drinks, then stares at the dissertation.* VICTOR *sets his drink down unobtrusively and untouched, and waits expectantly.* HOLMES *picks up the dissertation.*) A weighty tome.

VICTOR. I want it to be definitive.

HOLMES. If not inexhaustable. Katie says you have a publisher?

VICTOR. Yes. Just.

HOLMES. Congratulations.

VICTOR. But what do you think? Is it ready?

HOLMES. How long can you stay?

VICTOR. Till Sunday if need be.

HOLMES. Good. In that case I'd like to re-read it before I render judgement.

VICTOR. (*Disappointed.*) Oh. Well sure. (HOLMES *puts the manuscript down.*) Perhaps I could say a few words about what I'm trying to do. I develop the theme of the voice, disembodied if you will, calling to us from the wilderness. A voice full of hope for a new and better world.

HOLMES. Perhaps that's because he couldn't cope with this one.

VICTOR. Pardon?

HOLMES. Visionaries are easily embarassed, aren't they, Victor, by the untidiness of reality? (HE *pours himself another drink.*)

VICTOR. How do you mean?

HOLMES. The idealistic young have little tolerance for the toll life can take on their elders.

VICTOR. You mean Mrs. Bradford?

HOLMES. What?

VICTOR. You alluded just now to her drinking—

HOLMES. I did?

VICTOR. Is that why Wendel ran away?

HOLMES. That was the immediate cause I suppose. Things got pretty ugly around here. I practically had to live in my office during those years. But I don't want you to get the wrong idea about Katie. You should have seen her before Wendel was born, you wouldn't recognize the same woman. She was full of work, full of life. Then we got her pregnant in expectation of my getting tenure at Dartmouth, which I didn't because I wouldn't knuckle under to the tyranny of publish or perish. I preferred to spend my time with my students. I was Peck's Bad Boy. There was no hint then of my future glorious oeuvre. It wasn't till we were forced to emigrate to this backwater where there aren't any students to speak of anyhow that I began to write in earnest. Anyway the move, coming as it did on top of the pregnancy, left Katie debilitated. It was a hard birth and she never fully recovered. We took her to any number of doctors, the last of whom prescribed the then fashionable miracle drug: amphetamines.

VICTOR. Speed?

HOLMES. This was long before the invidious side effects were known. She became addicted to them and they eventually burnt her out. But she blamed herself for being weak because it never occurred to either of us that she was being poisoned. When Wendel was about eleven, medical research caught up with medical prescription and a new doctor took her off the drug cold turkey. But by then her strength was completely gone. She could barely mother and she'd had to stop working long since. So, she traded one dependance for another.

VICTOR. And Wendel?

HOLMES. He treated her with utter contempt. The very sight of her offended him. He was a moralistic little prig.

VICTOR. (*Distressed.*) And that's why he left?

HOLMES. In the middle of the night, without a word, in his sixteenth year . . . (HE *sees* VICTOR's *distress and takes rueful glee in adding:*) His final act was to steal a sum of money from Katie. The subject of your dissertation, your "Voice in the wilderness", financed his ascent of Parnassus with five hundred dollars she had saved for a washer-dryer to make her life a little easier.

VICTOR. But I don't understand, how could he be so callous knowing what she'd been through?

HOLMES. Well he didn't know the whole story. Not the amphetamine business that is.

VICTOR. Why not?

HOLMES. Katie didn't want him to feel responsible. Since it all started with his birth, you see.

VICTOR. So it would be fair to conclude that he might have left for his own survival?

HOLMES. What?

VICTOR. I mean from his point of view. If all he saw was the alcoholism with no idea of what led up to it.

HOLMES. (*Forcefully.*) If you want to talk about survivors, Victor, it's that woman. She sacrificed everything for him and his running away was like a judgement. But she reached down into herself and somewhere somehow found an ember that was still glowing. From the day he left she hasn't had a drop. She's been rebuilding her strength and you mark my words, she's determined to be again the woman she was.

VICTOR. . . . Sir, I do maintain that Wendel Bradford is our first major poetic voice in twenty years.

HOLMES. Yes?

VICTOR. Could you agree?

HOLMES. . . . This is a professional situation, Victor. I trust I am up to it.

VICTOR. I'm sorry, I didn't mean — It's just that, your opinion means a great deal to me.

HOLMES. I assure you that the father's eyes will not be blinded by the rising son.

VICTOR. (*Relieved.*) You had me worried.

HOLMES. No cause.

VICTOR. The thing is, you see, my publishers have suggested that if I could persuade you to write an introduction —

HOLMES. That *I* write an introduction? To my own son's work? That's a bit nepotistic isn't it?

VICTOR. It's an extraordinary opportunity. I mean it's

a unique situation. You're the preeminent scholar in the field and he's — maybe — our foremost young poet.

HOLMES. Almost a dynasty um? . . . Well an introduction would be a nice little modest something to get me started again. But you'd better let me read it again before I commit.

VICTOR. Fair enough. (KATIE *has reappeared, dressed, and carrying a tray with coffee, a pitcher of water, cups, and a water glass.* SHE *knocks.* HOLMES *quickly hides his liquor and pops a mint in his mouth.*) Entrez. (KATIE *pauses a moment before entering, something* SHE *always does as if to permit him time to make this adjustment.*) Katie?

KATIE. Excuse me.

HOLMES. Quite all right. (SHE *sets the tray on the desk.*) That water is for the crystals in my urine, those semi-precious stones of old age. Nurse Bradford sees to it I drink six glasses of water a day.

KATIE. (*Pouring a glass.*) Eight.

HOLMES. Eight. I find them all over the house lying in wait for me. Katie's memorized my movements and sets them in strategic locations. What time is it, hon? (HE *takes her wrist and looks at her watch.*) Um. Keep an eye out for John Ramsey. I left word for him to come see me at eleven-thirty. (VICTOR *glances at his watch.*) As Chairman of the Department it falls to me to tell him he's out of a job.

KATIE. You won't antagonize him, will you?

HOLMES. You don't have to worry, dear. I'll keep the peace.

KATIE. It's a shame he's so popular with the students.

HOLMES. That's precisely the problem. No one gets to be popular with these students, as you call them, without he sacrifice his academic integrity. This fellow,

Victor, his lectures are devoid of any content save gossip and anecdote and he grades like a man who needs friends desperately. He has an enormous following of followers who follow for the two following reasons: he wears tight, pre-faded blue jeans which give him that youthful testicle look the girlies like so much, and he's British, which the provincials here think is neat.

KATIE. Wouldn't it be easier for you if you just wrote him a letter?

HOLMES. We can't always do things the easiest way, can we. I'm sorry, Victor, but these distractions I have as Chairperson — as the unwed mothers on the faculty insist we be called — are endless. Let Katie fix you some lunch.

VICTOR. (*To* KATIE.) I'd rather go upstairs if I may and jot down some notes.

HOLMES. Upstairs?

VICTOR. Mrs. Bradford said I might use her studio.

HOLMES. Really? My compliments, Victor. I've been trying to coax her back up there for years.

KATIE. I told him it would be too cold.

HOLMES. Nonsense, you used to work up there year-round. (*To* VICTOR.) I'll will you my heater. (HE *unplugs the floor heater;* KATIE *intercepts it.*)

KATIE. Let me go up first, I'm sure it's terribly dusty. (SHE *exits.*)

HOLMES. Excellent, marvellous! And for my part I'll get to this in my next spare moment. (HE *indicates the dissertation as* HE *turns to check his calendar.*) Let's see . . . seminar, graduate committee, tennis — do you play tennis?

VICTOR. No.

HOLMES. Too bad. Well this afternoon is tight. I'll have another whack at it this evening. (HE *notices* VICTOR's *glass.*) You didn't touch your drink.

VICTOR. I don't drink.

HOLMES. (*Remembering this now; embarrassed.*) Oh.

VICTOR. (*Quickly.*) I'm sorry, I should have—

HOLMES. No no, more power to you. (HE *puts the glass behind the books with some chargrin, then with a covering smile:*) Actually that's something of a misnomer isn't it.

VICTOR. Pardon?

HOLMES. To call someone a Chairperson. It's discriminatory. It ought to be furniture-person. Or article-person.

VICTOR. Or vegetable-matter.

HOLMES. Or thing. That's it, the very word. Thing Bradford. That has a nice democratic ring to it, um? Can't offend anyone. (THEY *go into the living room.* HOLMES *bellows.*) Katie!?

VICTOR. I could find my own way—

HOLMES. No no, let her do it; it's good for her.

VICTOR. It's a real shame she had to stop painting.

HOLMES. Well that's something we don't talk about.

VICTOR. Is the rest of her work this good?

HOLMES. Other people said so. I never understood much about it, I just loved to see her working. She was a different person then.

VICTOR. She ought to have a show.

HOLMES. Oh god no. That's the last thing she wants.

VICTOR. I could arrange one.

HOLMES. You could? How?

VICTOR. My father has a gallery on Newbury Street.

HOLMES. In Boston?

VICTOR. Retrospectives are in now, especially for women.

HOLMES. Well it's an encouraging sign, isn't it, that she offered you her studio?

VICTOR. We used to exhibit her mother, but this is

better than anything Magda ever did.

HOLMES. (*Grinning.*) Oh for god's sake don't let Katie hear you say that. She was better and she knew it. Old Magda was a bitch on wheels. The resentment and competition between them was unbelievable. It still eats at Katie. To be exhibited in the same gallery—the perfection of it! There'd bound to be comparisons—in her favor. She'd love that. Ah—so that's how word of the Chair leaked out.

VICTOR. She told you? I'm sorry, I had no idea she didn't know.

HOLMES. It's all right, no harm done. I should have told her long ago. The thing is her health has been a problem for so long that any move before now was out of the question.

VICTOR. So it's for her sake then? I mean that's why—(HE *breaks off, embarrassed by his own question.*)

HOLMES. Why I'm still here at this cow college with a football team no one can beat and students who look more like basset hounds than anyone's children? Whose most sublime articulations are 'Y'know"? "I mean like far out"? Yes. But you know what scares me? Is how in the space of four short years they advance from that sub-cretin jibberish to words like "interface" and "self-actualization" and "beingness". The miracle that is modern education wreaks this transformation right under our very noses. It has been seriously suggested that we change the name of our department from English to Communications. My god, what will there be left to communicate? (KATIE *enters from upstairs, dust cloth in hand.*) Technology won't save us from this. It's up to us, Victor, you and me. We're right in the middle of it, son. (*A KNOCK at the front door.*) Ah. "Enter the Bastard." There's Ramsey. (KATIE *moves to admit him.*) Wait. I want him to knock twice.

KATIE. (*Chiding smile.*) Oh Holmes—

HOLMES. I want him to knock twice. (THEY *wait. Long pause. A second knock.*) Show him in. (HOLMES *goes into his study and sits at his desk to prepare himself for the interview.*)

KATIE. (*Opening the door.*) Hello. Oh. (*It is not* RAMSEY, *but a young boy.*)

STODDARD. (*With ingenous—if genuine—shyness.*) Is this the Dr. Bradford residence?

KATIE. Yes.

STODDARD. I'm a student with the university. Is Dr. Bradford in?

KATIE. Yes?

STODDARD. I wonder if I might have a minute of his time?

KATIE. Was he expecting you?

STODDARD. No ma'am, I'm a freshman.

KATIE. Come in. I'll see.

STODDARD. Thank you.

KATIE. Wait there.

STODDARD. Thank you.

KATIE. (*To* VICTOR, *as* SHE *crosses to study.*) Excuse me. (SHE *enters study;* HOLMES *swings around.*)

HOLMES. Well John—What's the matter?

KATIE. It's a student.

HOLMES. A student? What, a graduate student?

KATIE. A freshman.

HOLMES. What the hell's he doing here? Doesn't he know I have office hours?

KATIE. He seems anxious to see you.

HOLMES. Well I can't see him now.

KATIE. Why not?

HOLMES. Well—Ramsey's coming.

KATIE. I think it would be nice if you did.

HOLMES. Nice?

KATIE. Don't be such a snob.

HOLMES. I am not a snob!

KATIE. The final refuge of the teacher is to teach.

HOLMES. Don't quote me to myself!

KATIE. I'm sure it will only take a minute.

HOLMES. All right send him in. And when Ramsey comes he can damn well wait. (KATIE *returns to the living room;* HOLMES *busies himself opening his mail.*)

KATIE. He'll be happy to see you. (SHE *leads* VICTOR *upstairs.* STODDARD *crosses to open door and knocks.*)

HOLMES. (*Without looking up.*) Yes?

STODDARD. (*Stepping in.*) Dr. Bradford, sir? My name is Stoddard Oates, sir. (HOLMES *gives him a brief glance.*)

HOLMES. What can I do for you, Stoddard?

STODDARD. I wondered if it might be possible if I could transfer into your course.

HOLMES. Well God knows anything's possible; the seminar or the survey?

STODDARD. Uh—well I'm a freshman.

HOLMES. Of course, the survey then.

STODDARD. Yes, sir.

HOLMES. We're three weeks into the semester. The deadline for course changes was last Wednesday.

STODDARD. Yes, sir, I know.

HOLMES. What course do you want to drop?

STODDARD. Accounting 10b.

HOLMES. (HE *turns at this and gives* STODDARD *a closer look*.) Are you certain about that?

STODDARD. Yes, sir.

HOLMES. That goes against the grain of the currently fashionable mania, doesn't it?

STODDARD. I guess so.

HOLMES. (*Short pause.*) My course is not a gut, Mr. Oates. If you are after an easy grade, I suggest you look elsewhere.

STODDARD. I'm not after an easy grade, sir. (HOLMES *regards him.* HE *seems genuine.*)

HOLMES. In what do you intend to major?

STODDARD. Some kind of business.

HOLMES. Are you interested in poetry?

STODDARD. Yes, sir.

HOLMES. Why?

STODDARD. I don't know.

HOLMES. Where are you from?

STODDARD. Wynette.

HOLMES. What does your father do?

STODDARD. He's in agriculture.

HOLMES. Do you read much poetry on your own?

STODDARD. No, not a whole bunch.

HOLMES. Whence comes your interest?

STODDARD. Pardon?

HOLMES. Why do you want to transfer?

STODDARD. Oh I think it'd be good for me if I had some extra literature. I mean it's kind of hard for me just to read on my own.

HOLMES. Why don't you pick up the anthology we use, read some of the material and come see me during office hours tomorrow if you're still interested.

STODDARD. Well I really do want to transfer.

HOLMES. You're sure of that?

STODDARD. Yes sir. (*Short pause.*)

HOLMES. Sit down. (HE *does.* KATIE *re-appears from upstairs and goes off towards the kitchen.*) Have you ever read any poetry at all?

STODDARD. Yes, sir. Some of it was required in high school.

HOLMES. In other words no. Tell me, do you have any recollection of what you read? (*Pause.* STODDARD *thinks.*)

STODDARD. Uh-uh.

HOLMES. No lingering impressions? It didn't leave any kind of taste in your mouth?

STODDARD. Oh no, sir.

HOLMES. (*With increasing interest.*) A tabula rasa. That could be very interesting don't you think?

STODDARD. I look forward to whatever I can learn, sir.

HOLMES. How would you like to work directly with me? I won't assign you to a section, we'll meet once a week in a private tutorial.

STODDARD. You don't have to do that, sir.

HOLMES. No no, it would be an adventure for me too, to go back to the beginning and experience again through another's eyes that first excitement. We could read aloud to one another, what do you think?

STODDARD. I'm not classified as a remedial student.

HOLMES. (*Laughing.*) No no no, that's not what I meant at all. Let's see, forget the anthology. You say your father's a farmer? We'll start with Robert Frost. He was a farmer too, a New Englander, but I'm sure you'll recognize certain elements in his work right off: the indifference of Nature — no. No, I won't say a thing. Pick up his *Selected Poems* at the bookstore and just freefall into it. *Entre nous*, Stoddard, I've felt rather out of touch recently. I'll be genuinely interested in your impressions. We'll be equals, one man's opinion as valid as the next, hm? Oh — let me give you something — (HE *reaches down a slim volume.*) It's a volume of Frost's prose writing. He's a wonderful stylist, full of observation. (STODDARD *takes the book.*) Well, what do you say?

STODDARD. You'll let me transfer then?

HOLMES. Yes. Why, are you surprised?

STODDARD. Well yeah, I guess so.

HOLMES. I could see that. I think we'll get on quite well.

STODDARD. I mean I've heard they say you have a reputation for being real strict.

HOLMES. That's what you've heard, eh? Well it's true. This won't be easy. If anything you and I will work harder than the rest, read more, go deeper. You'll have to be on your toes; I'll grade you like a stranger. But I have a hunch—or what do you call it now? An impulse. Just as you did when you came here to the house.

STODDARD. Thank you, sir. (HE *rises.*) Could you give me a note?

HOLMES. Note?

STODDARD. Just saying you're letting me transfer.

HOLMES. Oh, not necessary. I'll sign your transfer slip. Do you have one?

STODDARD. Yes, sir.

HOLMES. (HE *signs it.*) Good. Just take this to the Registrar's Office. I'll call them right after lunch to confirm it. There. Well, son, we're in business. (HOLMES *offers his hand.* THEY *shake.*)

STODDARD. Thank you, sir. But I'd really like a note too, if that's all right.

HOLMES. Why?

STODDARD. I'd just sure appreciate it.

HOLMES. (*Smiles.*) You don't trust me eh? My reputation makes you suspicious?

STODDARD. Oh no, sir, it's not that at all.

HOLMES. No, Stoddard, I'm going to make you trust me. After all, if we're going to be up in front.

STODDARD. It ain't that I don't trust you, sir, really.

HOLMES. Then why? I don't understand. (*Pause.*)

STODDARD. Well you see, sir, I'm pledging the Sigma Nu Fraternity and I've been on probation all first semester. I mean that's standard, all the pledges are. And in order for us to get accepted we've all got to do something, you know, like one fellow had to give a speech on the Campus Corner in favor of women's rights and another had to throw a kind of epileptic fit in Carl's Ye Olde English Tavern. (*Pause.*)

HOLMES. And you had to get a note from me.

STODDARD. Well I didn't want to do any of that silly stuff.

HOLMES. I see. I didn't know my reputation was that potent. Then you really aren't interested in the course itself.

STODDARD. Oh yes, sir. The other part of the initiation's that I got to make a C-plus.

HOLMES. A C-plus.

STODDARD. So anyway that's why I need a note.

HOLMES. Why don't you just forge it?

STODDARD. I wouldn't do that. And you can bet I'll work hard. But it's okay if you just put me in a regular section. I ain't a remedial student. (*Pause.*)

HOLMES. What do you want me to say?

STODDARD. (*Shrugs.*) That Stoddard Oates has permission to transfer into English 60 I guess.

HOLMES. Would you like that on university letterhead?

STODDARD. It don't matter.

HOLMES. (*Writing.*) . . . permission . . . transfer . . . English 60 I guess.

STODDARD. Not the I guess, sir, that was just —

HOLMES. (*Holding out the paper.*) I have done precisely what you asked of me, Mr. Oates. That's what I'm here for. Here. (STODDARD *takes the paper, but sensing something wrong* HE *avoids* HOLMES' *eyes.*) May I have the book? (STODDARD *hands it back.*) I wonder if you're aware of the fact that you've just made a complete fool of me. You aren't, are you. You'll learn — you will learn a great deal at this university, but I'll wager very little of it will be in the classroom. Now if you'll excuse me, I have other things to do.

(STODDARD *hesitates, searching for an apology, but* HOLMES *has turned back to his desk and flipped open* VICTOR'S *dissertation.* STODDARD *leaves the study just as* KATIE *enters from the kitchen with* HOLMES' *lunch on a tray: sandwich and juice.*)

KATIE. Good day.

STODDARD. Good day, ma'am. (KATIE *pauses momentarily at* STODDARD'S *evident distress as* HE *leaves quickly, then goes to the study doorway.*)

KATIE. Holmes? (*At the sound of her voice* HE *slams the manuscript shut.*)

HOLMES. Where the hell is Ramsey? He's ten minutes late.

KATIE. (*Setting the lunch tray on his desk.*) Maybe he won't come.

HOLMES. Why not? I made myself perfectly clear.

KATIE. You've had a long day, you don't really want to deal with Ramsey now do you?

HOLMES. Long day, it's not even noon.

KATIE. Give me your coat, I think I can mend it now. (HOLMES *takes off his coat without rising.* KATIE *helps him.*)

KATIE. I wish you could relax more. All this tension's not good for you.

HOLMES. And when the hell am I going to learn to put these lenses in right?

KATIE. You'll get used to them, it's not important.

HOLMES. Don't say that, I hate that phrase.

KATIE. (*Smiles.*) I'm sorry. (SHE *gets her sewing kit from the side table.*)

HOLMES. I hate that one too. (HE *picks up a section of sandwich only to discover* HE *has no appetite.*) Why is it so cold in here?

KATIE. You gave Mr. Salt your heater.

HOLMES. Oh. (HE *tosses the sandwich down on the plate.*) I can't work here any more! (HE *does not move.* KATE, *seated at her table, registers his outburst.*)

KATIE. What did that boy want?

HOLMES. Wrong question.

KATIE. You'll feel better once you've eaten. Your blood sugar's low. (HOLMES *comes to the study door and watches her try to thread the needle. Her difficulty seems to calm him.*)

HOLMES. You want me to thread your needle?

KATIE. Please. Thank you, dear. (HOLMES *takes it and sits on the window seat where the light is good.*)

HOLMES. Things will be different when we get back east won't they? Do you ever think about those years before Wendel was born?

KATIE. No.

HOLMES. They were rare days of anarchy weren't they? When we did everything with verse and hunger? Remember when you had me paged during class because you were about to paint over that canvas and you needed someone to see it and tell you not to? (HE *is indicating the fourth wall.*) And me with my tenure hanging by a thread?

KATIE. I never should have done that. I'm sorry.

HOLMES. Nonsense. Do you think tenure at Dartmouth was more important than my first sight of this?

KATIE. Yes.

HOLMES. Well yes, maybe it was . . . That was the straw that broke the back of that fuddy duddy Chairman—what was his name?

KATIE. (*Smiling.*) Franklin Rich.

HOLMES. God he was a moribund old soul wasn't he?

Never wanted to turn out like him. No, we knew what mattered then. We had our priorities right. Of course, we ended up out here, but so what? I still get chills just looking at that. Your needle, madam. (HE *clicks his heels.*)

KATIE. Thank you, sir. (SHE *takes the needle,* HE *holds her hand.*)

HOLMES. There's a passion that still slumbers in these hands isn't there. "Sole Kate, to be beyond compare, never since the day we met has thy beauty so inflamed my sense." (HE *kisses her;* SHE *leans away with a smile.*)

KATIE. You've been eating those awful mints again.

HOLMES. I'm entitled to keep one pleasure aren't I? (*The mood lost,* HE *frees her hand and moves fretfully to the window as* SHE *begins to sew.*) Thank god we're almost out of here. We should have moved years ago.

KATIE. Wouldn't it be—oh I don't know—funny I suppose, if Wendel came home and didn't find us?

HOLMES. Why do you say that? It wouldn't be anything of the sort. Anyway he won't. I'm sure he'd consider a homecoming sentimental and regressive. He's a chapter closed. We agreed on that.

KATIE. Then why is that boy here?

HOLMES. Because I have an obligation. He asked for my help.

KATIE. When I saw him asleep in your study my first thought was that it was Wendel. It could have been, we don't know what he looks like anymore.

HOLMES. (HE *takes her wrist.*) What time is it? Uh. Bugger Ramsey. (HE *goes into the study and removes the books and notes from his morning class from his briefcase.*)

KATIE. He says he wants to talk to me about my life of all things.

HOLMES. Who does?

KATIE. Your Mr. Salt.

HOLMES. Well that makes sense. We are the boy's biological parents. You could field him this afternoon. I'm out till supper.

KATIE. . . . No.

HOLMES. Um?

KATIE. . . . I'd rather not.

HOLMES. What?

KATIE. I'd rather not.

HOLMES. (*Coming to the study door.*) Not what, talk to him? Why not?

KATIE. I'd just rather not be interviewed.

HOLMES. Why?

KATIE. He doesn't need to know about me does he?

HOLMES. That's not up to us to decide is it. Is something wrong? Are you not feeling well?

KATIE. I feel fine.

HOLMES. Would you rather do it tomorrow?

KATIE. No. I do not want him talking about me in his book. I don't want to be written about.

HOLMES. He's not writing about us, he's writing about Wendel. We're only footnotes for cnrist's sake.

KATIE. I know it's all the rage now for everyone to run to the nearest magazine or t.v. show to yammer on about themselves as if it mattered. I know candor and self-revelation are the supreme virtues of the day, but if you ask me it's indulent and undignified.

HOLMES. Victor's a scholar, not a yellow journalist.

KATIE. What's the difference?

HOLMES. What?

KATIE. I mean in this instance. It amounts to the same thing.

HOLMES. It does not. It's a question of intent. He's not trying to write a best-seller; it's a scholarly treatise. It's a matter of the literary historical record.

KATIE. It's a matter of my privacy. I'm none of his business.

HOLMES. Are you still angry at Wendel, is that it?

KATIE. No.

HOLMES. The lack of grace was his, not yours. You have nothing to apologize for.

KATIE. It's got nothing to do with Wendel!

HOLMES. Then we have an obligation—

KATIE. I have no more obligations!

HOLMES. Well thank god I still do! I know it's hard for you to accept, that something might be important, but Wendel is becoming a major literary figure whether we like it or not.

KATIE. I will not have Mr. Salt or anyone else drawing conclusions about my life!

HOLMES. Well I don't see how it will be possible to remain anonymous!

KATIE. Why? What have you told him?

HOLMES. Nothing! I haven't told him—(HE *stops, remembering that indeed* HE *has.*) Damnit! I don't understand. You're behaving like an eccentric old woman. I'm living with a crazy person. You've been sitting out here all these years going quietly mad right under my nose! This is the most extraordinary attitude I've ever beheld!

KATIE. (*Quieter.*) I know I'm being silly, but I've made my peace with things. The past is past and I don't want to go back into it. And I certainly don't want someone writing me down on paper. I don't want anything about me in any book, or any footnote. I want no record. When I die I want to be cremated and that's it. No headstone, no trace. And please don't look at me that way as if there was something wrong with me. I'm perfectly fine so long as you just don't worry about me. Here. (SHE *puts his jacket on the table and rises.*)

HOLMES. (*Shaken.*) Wait a minute—

KATIE. (*Putting her sewing kit away.*) Have your lunch.

HOLMES. Are you serious? Is that how you feel? Katie?

KATIE. I'm all right.

HOLMES. Of course you are! It'll all be different anyway once we've moved away from here. Once we're back east, once you go back to your work.

KATIE. What?

HOLMES. You'll see there's no reason to feel that way.

KATIE. Go back to what, painting? Whatever gave you that idea?

HOLMES. You did.

KATIE. I haven't given that a thought in years.

HOLMES. You stopped drinking.

KATIE. (*After the merest hesitation.*) I did that for Wendel.

HOLMES. Wendel? He was gone. He'd taken his five hundred dollar birthright and split.

KATIE. Still I did it for him, and for you.

HOLMES. Nonsense, you did it for yourself.

KATIE. I haven't painted in twenty years.

HOLMES. One doesn't lose a gift.

KATIE. It would only be therapy now.

HOLMES. Therapy?

KATIE. It's not something I need to do any more.

HOLMES. I don't believe you. Look at your hands, they're steady as a surgeon's.

KATIE. Yes for a few hours each day, but that's not enough. That's not nearly enough.

HOLMES. Then we'll go to a doctor.

KATIE. No.

HOLMES. Boston has the best specialists in the country.

KATIE. No. No more doctors. Why do you want to change things all around? I'm perfectly content.

HOLMES. Content? Teaching twelve-year-olds how to draw?

KATIE. Holmes, we don't talk about this.

HOLMES. Well it's time we did. People wanted your work, dealers did, museums!

KATIE. Stop it! Why does it matter to you what I do?

HOLMES. Because I thought I knew who I was living with!

KATIE. Well maybe you don't.

HOLMES. You had so much passion for your work — and for me. It's just the two of us now, again, the way it was.

KATIE. It's not the way it was and it can't be the way it was. Now stop all this. I have accepted things just as they are.

HOLMES. Buddhist claptrap!

(VICTOR *trots down the stairs and enters the living room in time to hear this last line.* HE *stops short, sensing the tension.*)

VICTOR. (*Forced smile.*) Hello again already. It *is* a little chilly up there — but it's okay, really. Clears the head . . . Just getting my jacket. (HE *goes into the study.*)

HOLMES. (*Between his teeth.*) Cheshire cat! Erasing!

KATIE. (*Controlling herself; quietly but firmly.*) Please do not make me angry.

(*A beat, then* HOLMES *turns abruptly on his heel and strides into the study to gather his breifcase and ten-nis bag.* HE *strides out of the study.*)

KATIE. Where're you going?

HOLMES. To class.

KATIE. What about Ramsey?

HOLMES. Ramsey isn't coming or haven't you figured that out yet. If that sonofabitch tries to make a scene over this he's going to have a fight on his hands, Chair or no Chair. (VICTOR *has come to the study doorway the better to eavesdrop, but keeps out of their sight.*) And I want you to talk to Victor.

KATIE. Why?

HOLMES. Because I want you to! I'm not going to discuss it. You're not going to fade out on me. We're not that old. We've got a good twenty-five years left if we play our cards right and that's a long, long time. ( HE *storms out.* VICTOR *appears in the study doorway.*)

KATIE. Forgive us, Victor. We don't usually carry on like that.

VICTOR. ( *Worried.* ) You have an objection to talking with me?

KATIE. . . . Yes. I do. (SHE *turns for her coat.*)

VICTOR. Why?

KATIE. I'm sure people will enjoy his work much more if they don't have to read all about me.

VICTOR. You could rely on my discretion.

KATIE. I'm sure I could but I'd rather not.

VICTOR. But I — I wouldn't make any mistakes, I've brought a tape recorder.

KATIE. I'm going shopping, do you have any requests for dinner?

VICTOR. Wait, please. What are the ground rules? What can I say?

KATIE. Nothing

VICTOR. "About Wendel's mother nothing is known."?

KATIE. Not even that. I'm sorry, I'm always the old stick in the mud it seems. Please don't take it personally, it's just me. My — eccentricities.

VICTOR. ( *A beat, then* HE *relaxes and smiles.* ) . . . I understand. So Wendel's desire for anonymity is something he inherited from you.

KATIE. . . . Excuse me I have to go. I have my coat on.

(SHE *exits.* VICTOR *looks after her then turns to the painting on the fourth wall as:*)

## LIGHTS GO TO BLACK

### SCENE THREE

*The following afternoon.*

HOLMES *is in the study with* JOHN RAMSEY. RAMSEY *has longish hair and moustache. HE wears tight, pre-faded blue jeans, a powder blue work shirt and a smart corduroy sports jacket with leather patches. On his feet are cowboy boots. HE is a man of thirty-nine trying to look twenty-six. HE holds a styrofoam coffee cup. Set nearby is a Burger King bag. It seems evident that this interview has gone on longer than* HOLMES *wanted, but for all his bravura in the previous scene* HE *seems concerned not to antagonize* RAMSEY.

RAMSEY. (*British accent.*) Anyway. That's that then isn't it. Finito. Nothing more to say, really. (*Pause.* HOLMES *does not look at him.*) But it's important to me, Holmes, that you know I'm not in the least surprised by the Department's hysterical decision to deny my tenure. I knew my student-oriented approach was bound to alienate some of the hectic little egos around here.

HOLMES. (*Uncomfortably.*) As I've said, John, if the Department's vote was unfair I'm sure the Deans will reverse it. In any case you have a year's period of grace.

RAMSEY. An ironic phrase that, isn't it.

HOLMES. Do you have the time?

RAMSEY. Three-thirty. Should I go?

HOLMES. If there's anything I can do please don't hesitate to ask.

RAMSEY. There is one thing.

HOLMES. Yes?

RAMSEY. What is your opinion of me?

HOLMES. Opinion?

RAMSEY. Yes.

HOLMES. I don't understand.

RAMSEY. Your personal opinion.

HOLMES. It was on my recommendation that you were hired here.

RAMSEY. Yes, but I mean now.

HOLMES. The situation's out of our hands now.

RAMSEY. I simply want to know what you think of me.

HOLMES. I hope you don't think I bear you any ill will.

RAMSEY. Quite frankly I don't know what to think. For all I can tell I'm standing here making an ass of myself trying to talk to a man who despises me. (HOLMES *makes no protest.* VICTOR *appears from upstairs carrying his attache case and an old shoebox along with a small stack of snapshots. Hearing* RAMSEY'S *voice,* HE *stops, glances at his watch and sits on the Windsor settee to wait.*) I only came to this Heidelberg on the Yazoo because of you.

HOLMES. I know. We got on very well at first didn't we?

RAMSEY. Got on? You were bloody radiant. You all but promised me tenure.

HOLMES. I had no right to do that, John. I'm sorry.

RAMSEY. *You're* sorry?

HOLMES. I thought we'd become closer colleagues than we did. I honestly wanted that. (HE *opens the door; both men leave the study.* VICTOR *rises.*)

VICTOR. Time?

HOLMES. Oh—yes.

RAMSEY. Hello.

HOLMES. Oh—Victor, this is John Ramsey. Victor Salt.

RAMSEY. How do you do.

HOLMES. (*To* VICTOR.) John was just going.

RAMSEY. Are you here to interview for a job?

HOLMES. He's done a dissertation on my boy's poetry.

RAMSEY. Ah, you're modern then.

HOLMES. Wait for me in the study, would you, Victor. I'll just be a moment.

VICTOR. Certainly. Oh—I asked Mrs. Bradford if I could take the two of you to dinner tonight.

HOLMES. That's very nice, thank you.

VICTOR. Well—she said she didn't want to put me out.

HOLMES. What the hell did she mean by that, we'd love to go.

RAMSEY. (*Jumping in.*) May I suggest a new Greek restaurant I discovered on Shawnee Street? They serve the classical moussaka without the sauce. Their wine list still leaves something to be desired, but they do have one or two fair Bordeaux if you can stomach a red with Greek food. (HE *smiles at* VICTOR.) I expect you'll be happy if Wendel walks off with the Pulitzer this year won't you.

VICTOR. Very happy.

RAMSEY. Wendel's quite the rage now isn't he. I'm sorry I'm not more familiar with his work. I prefer westerns and murder mysteries myself. (*Short pause.*) Well, is his dissertation any good?

VICTOR. Excuse me.

HOLMES. Yes. Thank you.

VICTOR. Oh—what's the name of that Greek restaurant?

RAMSEY. The Little Colonel.

VICTOR. Thanks. (*VICTOR goes into study and closes door. HE looks for a phone book, and sits at desk to look up and jot down some numbers from the Yellow Pages.*)

RAMSEY. He seems the eager sort. Certainly made the clever move coming to see you.

HOLMES. (*Evenly.*) That's one of the better young scholars in the country, he doesn't need to brown-nose me.

RAMSEY. I'm sure not. His dissertation is good then?

HOLMES. Oh yes.

RAMSEY. Still no idea where Wendel is?

HOLMES. No.

RAMSEY. That's too bad. Caroline and I have decided against having children.

HOLMES. That seems to be the common wisdom of the age.

RAMSEY. She doesn't want to give up her pottery.

HOLMES. I really must excuse myself, John.

RAMSEY. Of course . . . I'm sorry you feel there's nothing to be done.

HOLMES. (*Rising to the bait in RAMSEY's tone.*) We're not going to have any trouble are we?

RAMSEY. Trouble?

HOLMES. You're very popular, you know that. You don't have to prove it.

RAMSEY. Yes.

HOLMES. And you know students, any cause in a calm.

RAMSEY. Well they are the ones affected by this aren't they?

HOLMES. I'm under a lot of strain at the moment, John: the operations on my eyes, that fellow in there—

RAMSEY. Not to mention the Chair at Brandeis. (HE *smiles.*) Which you hear about tomorrow.

HOLMES. How do you know that?

RAMSEY. I fully appreciate your situation. Your nerves must be stretched to their limits.

HOLMES. Yes, frankly, John, they are. You can see why I'd appreciate not having any sort of fuss. It really wouldn't help your case any.

RAMSEY. Of course not. Mere revenge.

HOLMES. So. I have your word?

RAMSEY. My word?

HOLMES. Just for my own peace of mind.

RAMSEY. That's a bit old-fashioned isn't it?

HOLMES. We're both gentlemen, John.

RAMSEY. You don't really mean that. (*Short pause.*) The fact is, I'm afraid word may have already slipped out.

HOLMES. How? You mentioned it in class?

RAMSEY. The subject came up and I—

HOLMES. Your subject is Elizabethan Literature, John.

RAMSEY. I could help you, Holmes. We could help each other. I happen to know that the Department's vote was close—

HOLMES. How? That was confidential—

RAMSEY. Oh don't be such an old fuddy-duddy. I asked someone and he told me. The point is, I know that on a close vote the Deans give a great deal of weight to the Chairperson's recommendation.

HOLMES. . . . I see. And that's why my personal opinion of you was so important.

RAMSEY. I can stop anything the students might be planning.

HOLMES. (*Outraged.*) Just what are you suggesting?

RAMSEY. (*Losing his cool.*) Why don't you like me anymore? What is it I do that's so wrong? I'll give you my word there'll be no trouble, but you must tell me, please.

HOLMES. (*Quietly.*) I've been giving my opinion here for twenty-three years to no perceptible avail. I'm tired of giving it.

RAMSEY. Well bully for you! Where am I supposed to get another job? It's all very well for you, you're off to become an emeritus old fart. At least I can relate to my students, we have a bit of fun, is that such a crime? I won't let this go without a fight.

HOLMES. If you feel the need to head up a children's crusade, by all means go ahead.

RAMSEY. You're damn right I will.

HOLMES. I won't give you the satisfaction of fighting back.

RAMSEY. I don't give a sparrow's tit what you do. You're out of touch, mister, you're hopelessly out of touch. When I talk to you my feet fall asleep. You know what your students say about you behind your back? Boring! (HE *goes.* HOLMES *strides angrily into the study and goes straight for the whiskey.* VICTOR *rises.*)

VICTOR. You must be glad that's over.

HOLMES. (*Pouring a drink.*) It isn't. Victor, let me give you a piece of advice: don't ever be deceived by charm. Sit down, it's too crowded in here if we both stand. (VICTOR *sits.* HE *opens his attache case and takes out notebook and tape recorder.*)

VICTOR. Well. Shall we move on to happier waters?

HOLMES. What?

VICTOR. Will it be okay if I tape our discussion?

HOLMES. I've no objection—but I'm afraid I'm not ready quite—(HE *breaks off.*)

VICTOR. Oh.

HOLMES. That fellow Ramsey stayed longer than I expected. I need to organize my— Give me the rest of the afternoon, would you?

VICTOR. Sure. (*Forced smile.*) Another reprieve.

HOLMES. Thanks. I seem to have trouble—finishing sentences. I—(HE *breaks off.*)

VICTOR. I did want to ask you about these.

HOLMES. Uh?

VICTOR. Some old photographs. I found them in the studio.

HOLMES. Oh? (HE *takes the proffered photographs.*)

VICTOR. (*Indicating the top one.*) Is that Mrs. Bradford?

HOLMES. Yes. (HE *grins.*) I took this in the White Mountains shortly after we were married.

VICTOR. It's very good.

HOLMES. Well I was something of a camera buff then. (HE *leafs through the rest of them.*) Good golly I'd forgotten all about these.

VICTOR. She's very attractive.

HOLMES. I always said Katie had a pact with the devil.

VICTOR. (*Holding up a snapshot* HE *kept separate.*) And this is Wendel?

HOLMES. Yes. You can tell by the sneer. (*A beat.*) What exactly did she say to you?

VICTOR. Mrs. Bradford?

HOLMES. When you asked her about dinner tonight?

VICTOR. She said she's always too tired to do anything in the evenings.

HOLMES. Because of her insomnia?

VICTOR. Yes. She—

HOLMES. That's just an excuse. Oh I know it's a habit now, but it's ridiculous. She retires early, sleeps late, and in between she sits up half the night out there in her chair. We barely see each other any more. (HE *hands the photographs back*.) What about them?

VICTOR. I wondered if I might get some of these reproduced for the book.

HOLMES. Snapshots in a scholarly treatise?

VICTOR. My agent says that even ten photographs opens up a whole new market.

HOLMES. Agent? You have an agent?

VICTOR. She's terrific.

HOLMES. (*Dubiously*.) Oh. Well I don't know, if you think it's proper—

VICTOR. Thanks. (HE *puts the snapshots back in the box*.)

HOLMES. But I think you ought to get Katie's permission as well.

VICTOR. Sure. (HOLMES *turns to the door*.) Will that be a problem?

HOLMES. Why?

VICTOR. She seems to be against this whole enterprise.

HOLMES. Did she talk to you?

VICTOR. No, she refused to. She treats me as if I were from *People* Magazine.

HOLMES. I'm sorry, Victor. I agree you ought to have a free hand. The principle of—

VICTOR. Well her silence would make it very difficult for me, to say the least. I think she's the key to our understanding of Wendel's poetry.

HOLMES. Oh?

VICTOR. Don't you see it?

HOLMES. I—hadn't considered it in that—light, I—

VICTOR. I think he's obcessed with her. I think the entire thrust of his philosophy keys off his feelings for her. I don't understand what the problem is.

(KATIE *enters by the front door, dressed in a plain over-*

*coat and scarf.* SHE *carries a Mexican straw bag filled with dried grasses, leaves, etc.* SHE *removes her coat and scarf in the foyer.*)

HOLMES. (*Trying to reason it out.*) Well, she's embarrassed. She sees herself as a failure. I didn't realize this.

VICTOR. Well I would certainly like her to feel she could speak freely to me. Could you ask her again?

HOLMES. I—think this ought to be between you and her.

VICTOR. And if she still says no?

HOLMES. Well you're a clever fellow—

VICTOR. I mean what are the ethics of the situation?

HOLMES. Ethics?

VICTOR. You've already told me a great deal. More, I'm sure, than she wants me to know.

HOLMES. Oh for god's sake don't let her know I blabbed all that. I had no idea she'd— Just try to persuade her she's important, she counts. She just needs to get her confidence back is all. You're a charming lad, I'm sure you can do it. It'll just take time and patience on both our parts. (MEN *react to a noise from the living room:* KATIE, *sitting at her table with the straw bag, scrapes her chair.* HOLMES *hides his glass and pops a mint in his mouth. Then, holding up a finger to* VICTOR, HE *opens the study door.*) You're back.

KATIE. (*Startled.*) Yes. (SHE *rises and moves about the room to get two of the vases. When* SHE *turns back to her table* SHE *sees that both* MEN *have entered the room.*) Are you finished already?

HOLMES. For now, yes. Where've you been?

KATIE. (SHE *picks up on the veiled edge in his voice as* SHE *continues to divert herself with her task.*) In the fields south of town. Near the river. My usual haunt.

HOLMES. More weeds? When we move we'll have to hack our way our of here with machetes.

KATIE. (*Countering.*) I saw Ramsey leaving. I hope he hasn't tired you.

HOLMES. (*With faint sarcasm.*) No he hasn't tired me, dear. I'm still standing.

KATIE. Is he going to cause trouble?

HOLMES.  . . . Did he say anything to you?

KATIE. No. I pretended not to see him.

HOLMES. "Pretended not to see him." If only life were that simple. . . . No. There's not going to be any trouble. You don't have to fret.

KATIE. That's a relief.

HOLMES. If it weren't for Katie's example of unparallelled restraint, I'd still be insufferably outspoken, wouldn't I? I'd still be Peck's Bad Boy.

KATIE. That would look a bit silly at your age.

HOLMES. Katie, Victor's asked us out to dinner.

KATIE. Oh. How nice.

HOLMES. I want us to go.

KATIE. Of course.

VICTOR. (*To her.*) Good. Shall I make a reservation?

|  | KATIE | ) |
| No. |  | ) |
|  | HOLMES | ) |
| Yes. |  | ) |

(*A beat.*)

HOLMES. Excuse me. I have work to do. I'll leave you. (HE *exchanges a brief look with* VICTOR, *then shuts himself in his study and, after a moment, sits to confront the manuscript.* KATIE *busies herself with her new arrangements.*)

VICTOR. I read your local paper this morning. It says they've forecast snow for tonight.

KATIE. Really?

VICTOR. Snow must be rare here.

KATIE. It is.

VICTOR. It must bring back memories.

KATIE. No. Did you find the high school this morning despite my directions?

VICTOR. Oh yes. (HE *smiles, takes out a notebook and refers to it.*) His English teacher said he was arrogant, his math teacher found him inattentive, and his phys. ed. instructor called him an uncoordinated loner. The most arresting image came from his French teacher, she likened him to Rimbaud — in everything that is, but his command to French.

KATIE. (SHE *smiles.*) He wasn't a student. That used to upset Holmes.

VICTOR. Oh? (HE *waits for more.* KATIE *says nothing.*) Dr. Bradford said I should ask you about these.

KATIE. (*Unlike* HOLMES, SHE *recognizes the box at once.*) Where did you find those?

VICTOR. Upstairs. I'd like to get a couple of them reproduced for the book.

KATIE. What did Holmes say?

VICTOR. He thinks it's a good idea.

KATIE. Is that where you're off to now?

VICTOR. (*Hesitantly.*) Well yes, unless --

KATIE. Please don't let me stop you.

VICTOR. Can I use a picture of you?

KATIE. No.

VICTOR. There are some lovely ones that your husband took —

KATIE. No.

VICTOR. . . . I think you have less vanity than anyone else I've ever met.

KATIE. I'm sorry.

VICTOR. I've asked Dr. Bradford if he'd write an introduction for the book. I'd love to use one of your paintings for the dust jacket.

KATIE. I'd rather you didn't consider that.

VICTOR. To make it a family endeavor?

KATIE. No. I'm sorry.

VICTOR. I really do need to talk to you, Mrs. Bradford. May I at least try to explain why? (*A beat, then* KATIE *pauses in her work and sits to let him have his say.*) You're very important to me. You're far more important than perhaps you realize. You see, there's an astonishing impulse behind Wendel's writing. He's torn between two extremes: faith and terror. I was able to identify his tension early on, it fascinated me. But what I had no way of knowing was the source. Where did it come from? I think I've found it now, Mrs. Bradford. It's you. Your son's poetry is full of the most sublime form of hedonism: he believes we are capable of everything our theologies and philosophies have hinted at. But he is also haunted by the knowledge of how fragile the life force really is. He knows for all our possibilities how easily we can become victims.

KATIE. I thought I made myself clear yesterday, Mr. Salt.

VICTOR. I think you're wrong to feel the way you do about yourself.

KATIE. How I feel about myself is none of your business. Now you'd better go, the stores close early around here.

VICTOR. (*Tight-lipped.*) All right. (HE *gets his coat.*) Can I ask you just one question? Why are you destroying your paintings? They're just stacked up there without protection in an unheated attic. That is valuable work, you must know that. I understand the problems of an interrupted career, but what I don't understand is your indifference to your not inconsiderable achievement.

KATIE. What I have *done*, Victor, has no meaning for me. But perhaps you're too young to understand that.

VICTOR. So I'm wrong—you do have vanity.

KATIE. (*To end the discussion:*) I don't paint anymore because I have a nervous condition that causes my hands to tremble.

VICTOR. . . . I'm sorry, I didn't know that.

KATIE. There are a lot of things you don't know.

VICTOR. That's why I'm here.

KATIE. Mr. Salt, you came here because you need my husband's help. I assume you realize for that you need his good will. Now I trust you won't approach me on this matter again.

VICTOR. No. I don't hate much, Mrs. Bradford, but I do hate waste — of any sort.

(VICTOR *turns on his heel and goes.* KATIE *picks up a leaf from her table and crushes it.* HOLMES, *hearing the outdoor slam, flips the dissertation shut in frustration.* HE *rises and goes into the living room.*)

HOLMES. The bastard's handcuffed me.

KATIE. Victor?

HOLMES. Wendel. Do you think he's done this deliberately?

KATIE. What?

HOLMES. Become famous. It's a brilliant refinement on the old Oedipal battle isn't it.

KATIE. What's wrong?

HOLMES. I can't read that dissertation.

KATIE. Why not?

HOLMES. My eyes won't focus. My mind won't focus. I can't form an opinion.

KATIE. Why don't you lie down?

HOLMES. Oh for god's sake.

KATIE. If it's that difficult do you have to do it?

HOLMES. That would be your solution wouldn't it, like dinner?

KATIE. What?

HOLMES. A house guest takes his hosts to dinner, it's a

perfectly normal thing to do. If you can't even handle that what are you going to do when we move? It's not going to be like here; people think I'm a widower. There'll be social functions, we'll be expected to entertain. We have old friends there.

KATIE. Who will want to know what I've been doing with myself?

HOLMES. I wrote a letter this morning to Jerry MacKay, my old friend at Harvard. I asked him to scout up the best neurologist in the Boston area.

KATIE. For me?

HOLMES. Yes.

KATIE. Where is it?

HOLMES. Already in the mail.

KATIE. You had no right to do that.

HOLMES. I'm not going to stand idly by and watch you just wait out your time.

KATIE. Well you won't have to. I'm not going.

HOLMES. Not going where?

KATIE. To Boston.

HOLMES. What's that, a joke?

KATIE. No.

HOLMES. Of course you're going, what else would you do? Let's try to stick to reality okay? We have enough trouble with that without skittering off on irrational tangents.

KATIE. I won't lie and pretend I've given this a great deal of thought. I didn't intend to say that. It sounds awful. I'm shocked. But I also know it's the right thing.

HOLMES. Why?

KATIE. I won't have you looking at me reproachfully for the rest of my life.

HOLMES. I'm not reproachful, you're just so damn negative!

KATIE. You watch me. Is she ready yet? Is today the

day? I hate being watched.

HOLMES. Then admit you're own strength! Look how you overcame the drinking. (*Short pause.*)

KATIE. (*Quietly.*) I couldn't have done that without you.

HOLMES. Me? What did I do?

KATIE. You forbade liquor in the house. You set an example by stopping too. (*The double lie hangs in the air between them for a moment, then:*)

HOLMES. (*Quietly.*) I see. You don't want your strength back, is that it?

KATIE. I have the strength I need. There is a stillness at the center of things, a peace. That makes everything bearable and even beautiful in a way. I have found the strength to achieve that calm—

HOLMES. Calm? That's catatonia!

KATIE. —but obviously that's a disappointment to you, (*Her voice rising.*) and I cannot stand your disapproval!

HOLMES. (*His voice rising.*) Ambition is foolish in the old?

KATIE. We simply do not understand each other anymore, that's all. And there is no earthly or unearthly reason why we should stay together. I'll pay you for the house.

HOLMES. What?

KATIE. I'll get a job and pay you for it. (SHE *is close to tears.*) I can do that much. I want to do that much.

HOLMES. What the hell are you talking about?

KATIE. I know you've been unhappy here and I've felt guilty that it's my fault. So I'm very excited for you, you mustn't think I'm not. I think it's wonderful that you're getting the honor you deserve. I'm so relieved.

HOLMES. Are you. That's very nice, dear. I must say I

had anticipated any number of reactions to this appointment, but frankly relief wasn't one of them. All right stay here then. Wait for Wendel to come home. Embrace your living death. I've got work to do! Finito! (HE *strides into the study and slams the door.*)

## LIGHTS GO TO BLACK

### SCENE FOUR

*Late that same night.*
*The house is in darkness; only the front pourch light is on. After a moment, the sounds of* HOLMES *and* VICTOR *returning from dinner.* HOLMES *is quite drunk.*

HOLMES. (*Stumbling.*) Agh! (THEY *enter the house,* VICTOR *helping him.*) Damn pourch light, it's enough to blind you. (HOLMES *snaps it off.*) That's better. Cold eh? (VICTOR *assists him into the living room, sits him down on the window seat.*) We may get a little snow tonight, fancy that. Am I sitting down?

VICTOR. (*With suppressed anger.*) Yes.

HOLMES. Good. Where were we?

VICTOR. Nowhere.

HOLMES. Huh. I thought it felt familiar . . . (VICTOR *goes into the study, flings down his tape recorder then takes off his trenchcoat.* HE *sits on the cot and in the darkness slowly begins to undress.* HOLMES, *oblivious, continues to talk.*) Did I tell you about this house? It was Katie's idea. She fell in love with the view, she had to have it. It stood in the middle of a wheat field, the town was a mile away in those days. Hard to imagine that now, eh? . . . Did I tell you how we met? It was during the war, my first job out of Harvard, my first exile, Colby College in Maine. I was teaching Shakespeare and Milton to boys in uniform. They were the best students I ever had. They knew it was absurd, reading poetry before going off to war, but they wanted to take something with them, they wanted to hear those words. I'd read aloud, and their faces, you should have seen their faces. Then one day there was a new face in the back of the room. She'd been in Paris on an art scholarship. She'd had to come home because of the war. I assumed she was there for the troops, but it was for me, to listen to me read. "And what would you? Make me a willow cabin at your gate and call upon my soul within the house . . ." Even then, she had a way of making herself almost invisible. Then one day after class she approached me: her father was ill, would I come out to the farm and read to him? . . . It was perfect . . . Victor? . . . Victor? (HE *rises and staggers into the study.* HE *turns on the lamp.*) What are you doing?

VICTOR. Getting ready for bed.

HOLMES. We can't go to bed this early, it's not midnight yet. How 'bout a nightcap?

VICTOR. I don't drink.

HOLMES. I know, I know, just keep me company. (*Going to bookcase for glasses,* HE *sees* KATIE *has set out his pitcher of water.*) Look — isn't this thoughtful. Have a glass of water then.

VICTOR. No thanks. I might piss myself in my sleep.

HOLMES. (*Pouring a glass.*) Help me fill my quota.

VICTOR. I'm very full.

HOLMES. I'd cripple myself for life trying to get all this water through my system. (HE *advances on* VICTOR *with the glass.*) Come on. (HE *stumbles. The water spills.* VICTOR *grabs the glass from him and puts it down.*) We'll be partners in duplicity. (HE *turns on the tape recorder.*) "Partners in duplicity." (VICTOR *grabs the machine and shuts it off.*)

VICTOR. I'm really pretty tired, sir.

HOLMES. Oh don't go to bed yet. (HE *grins and wipes some water from his coat.*) These clothes are a disgrace. I'm sixty-two years old and I look like a bohemian. Katie and I were bohemians once, did I tell you? She used to whistle, can you imagine that? (VICTOR *starts to exit with his shaving kit.*) Where are you going?

VICTOR. You already told me that.

HOLMES. (*Suddenly angry.*) What's the matter!

VICTOR. Nothing, I'm tired that's all.

HOLMES. You're upset because I haven't finished your dissertation?

VICTOR. I'm sorry I put you on the spot.

HOLMES. Don't flatter yourself. (VICTOR *goes into the living room.* HOLMES *follows.*) You want to know what I think of Wendel's poetry? It's brilliant—like a diamond, glittering and cold as stone. It shows a want of human feeling. Oh it's very modern, very—what's the word?—alienated. But it's dead. It's dead.

VICTOR. (*Challenged.*) He writes about salvation and loss and—

HOLMES. He writes about salvation because he doesn't have anything else to write about.

VICTOR. How do you know that?

HOLMES. He doesn't know what life is all about. He's too young!

VICTOR. And you have the patent on wisdom? (KATIE *enters in her bathrobe.* SHE *turns on the overhead light.* HOLMES *blinks.*)

KATIE. Holmes?

HOLMES. Who's that?

KATIE. Are you all right?

HOLMES. (*Looking right at her.*) Is someone here? Victor, do you see anyone?

KATIE. What's wrong?

HOLMES. Nothing's wrong. Why do you always assume something is wrong?

KATIE. You don't look well, was it that Greek food?

HOLMES. No is wasn't the food, I'm drunk.

KATIE. You should go straight to bed then.

HOLMES. I'm drunk! Victor, tell her: did I get sick or did I get sick?

KATIE. Did he?

VICTOR. In the restaurant.

HOLMES. I'm all right now. (HE *grins.*) We just have to remember not to go back to that restaurant.

KATIE. (*Taking charge.*) Sit down. (SHE *guides him to the Windsor settee and sits him down. Then* SHE *goes into the study and pours a glass of water.*)

HOLMES. Of course you don't want me drawing attention to us, do you, since you're planning to stay here. Something in the air here agrees with her, Victor, the chloroform I think.

KATIE. (*Returning to him.*) You should have some water.

HOLMES. (*Waving it away.*) Of fuck water!

KATIE. To dilute the alcohol in your stomach.

HOLMES. Ah! The voice of experience.

KATIE. You're not used to it.

HOLMES. I'm not? (HOLMES *rises and goes into the*

*study.*)

KATIE. Can you undress yourself?

HOLMES. I'm *not*? (HE *sweeps the books from the shelf where the liquor is kept.*) What do you call this? I've got a distillery in here. I've got the whole goddamned state of Kentucky in here!

KATIE. (*Refusing to be goaded.*) Let's get you to bed then.

HOLMES. Why don't you come with me?

KATIE. Give me your arm.

HOLMES. (*Breaking away.*) I can find my own way. Half a life and half a wife.

KATIE. Victor, would you please leave us alone?

HOLMES. Wait a minute! Weren't you two supposed to have a talk?

KATIE. We did. This afternoon.

HOLMES. Oh? Victor, is this true? Victor? (VICTOR, *not wanting to be drawn in, moves away.* HOLMES *turns back to* KATIE *in the study and holds out the bottle.*) How about a drink? Come on, to loosen the old tongue, get the old memory juices flowing?

KATIE. (*Controlled, not wanting to rile him further.*) No thank you.

HOLMES. Why not? Afraid you might remember when you still had some life in you? You knew about this all along didn't you? You knew I hadn't kept my end of the bargain and you never said a word.

KATIE. It wasn't necessary for you to stop too.

HOLMES. No, of course not. You didn't need me, you never needed me. I just got in the way. I just dragged you from one doctor to another and made you take their stinking speed of departed memory when all you wanted was to be left alone.

KATIE. I don't blame you for that.

HOLMES. I wish you would, at least it would show some feeling for me! Why didn't you want Wendel to know what had happened to you?

KATIE. I didn't want him to feel responsible.

HOLMES. No! No! The truth is you didn't want to include him in your life.

KATIE. That's not true!

HOLMES. It is! You didn't want him to know anything that might have drawn him close to you. He was never part of what mattered to you and neither was I.

KATIE. That's not true! I loved Wendel! How dare you hold that bottle out to me, what do you think I am? Of course I loved Wendel. He left because I paid him to go. I gave him that five hundred dollars.

HOLMES. Don't make up lies for him!

KATIE. He didn't steal it, I gave it to him. I made him go because I was sick and tired of his contempt. It was choking me! I didn't know what else to do, my brain wasn't right. I thought it was the only chance I had . . . (*With a kind of horrible triumph.*) And it worked. It worked . . . I woke up the next morning and I stood in the doorway of his empty room and I knew what I had done. And I stopped drinking.

HOLMES. Telling him the truth never occurred to you?

KATIE. What truth? Can you honestly tell me what the truth is?

HOLMES. The pills?

KATIE. The pills. I'm sick and tired of hearing about the pills. It has nothing to do with reasons. I don't know what the reasons are, I only know what happened. Wendel wanted to go, he was ready to go. He only needed someone to say yes, go, it's all right.

HOLMES. How do you know that?

KATIE. Because he was tired of picking me up when I fell. He was tired of the phone calls.

HOLMES. What phone calls?

KATIE. He'd come home from school and the phone

would be ringing. "We've got a woman here . . ."

HOLMES. What? Where?

KATIE. You'd be amazed how many bars there are in one mid-sized town. . . . Wendel had to go. I could feel his spirit hardening in judgement and shame. I knew I had to free him, that was the only thing I could still do for him. The money was simply the last thing I had to give.

HOLMES. I never knew about this!

KATIE. How could you? You were always in your office, day and night, working on your great scholarly tomes.

HOLMES. (*Challenged, angrily.*) Was I? I gave you every encouragement!

KATIE. (*Bitterly.*) Yes I know, you never stood in my way, did you. You even built me the studio rather than furnish the second floor. First Mother wanted me to be perfect, then you wanted me to be perfect, so I took the pills and tried to do it all . . . Then I became ill, and you became distant. You were terrified by my failure weren't you. (*Brief pause.*)

HOLMES. (*Holding himself together with a covering sarcasm.*) I see. Very nice. Very neat. Well, we'll start over again tomorrow. (HE *sheds his coat in a heap at the foot of the stairs and staggers off to bed.* KATIE *bends to gather up the books.* VICTOR *comes to the study door.*)

VICTOR. Are you okay?

KATIE. (*Startled, turns.*) Yes. Everything's fine.

VICTOR. I tried to stop him from ordering the second bottle of wine. I don't drink, that was the problem. (*Pause.*) I see now why they encourage us to write dissertations on dead people (*Short pause.*) I've decided to leave tomorrow morning. You'll be glad to hear that.

KATIE. Was Holmes able to give you the help you wanted?

VICTOR. Frankly no.

KATIE. I'm sorry. He really is a wonderful teacher. I hope you won't think badly of him.

VICTOR. I won't pretend I'm not disappointed, but I believe I understand. He can't forgive Wendel for breaking up his love affair with you.

KATIE. (SHE *hadn't expected that.*) Oh god . . .

VICTOR. You're not going with him back East?

KATIE. (*Realizing.*) You — you overheard all that?

VICTOR. I couldn't very well help it.

KATIE. Of course. Well, I guess you see now why I don't want to be written about.

VICTOR. Yes. I do.

(*Neither moves as:*)


LIGHTS GO TO BLACK


SCENE FIVE

*In darkness we hear:*

VICTOR. Yes sir.

LIGHTS UP.

*It is early the following morning. The living room is filled with early light; the study is illuminated by* HOLMES' *lamp.* VICTOR'S *suitcase and attache case lie open on the cot.* VICTOR, *partly dressed, sits in the swivel chair, his stockinged feet on the desk.* HE *is talking into the phone.*

VICTOR. I agree, I think that's the best way to proceed under the circumstances . . . Yes I know, but frankly I think we'll be better off without it. Anyway that's why I called . . . Yes, I can be in New York by tomorrow evening . . . (HE *smiles.*) I know, but I find travel a waste of time . . . Yes sir, till then.

(HE *hangs up and sits for a long moment, brooding.* HE *rouses himself with a small sigh and continues to dress.*

HOLMES *appears from upstairs.* HE *is dressed in a three-piece suit and moves with the special care of one hung-over.* HE *goes to the front door, opens it and bends down for the morning student paper, which is rolled up and bound with a rubber band.* HE *shuts the door.*

VICTOR *reacts to the noise of the door and quickly begins to pack his suitcase.*

HOLMES *crosses to the study door, composes himself, and KNOCKS.*)

HOLMES. Victor?
VICTOR. Yes?
HOLMES. May I come in?
VICTOR. Just a minute.

(VICTOR *takes the manuscript from the desk and puts it in his attache case and snaps it shut.* HE *adjusts his clothes and smoothes his hair.*

*Meanwhile* KATIE *enters dressed in skirt and blouse.* SHE *crosses to the window seat and takes out a port-*

*folio case.* SHE *turns to her table and sees* HOLMES.
THEY *speak to each other in muted tones.*)

KATIE. I heard the door, I thought you'd gone.

HOLMES. No, just the paper. You're up early.

KATIE. (*At her table, putting the poster in the port-folio case.*) I'm going to the printers, I'll be there most of the day. (*Referring to his suit.*) Why are you wearing that?

HOLMES. I need something extra to hold me together today. I hear from Brandeis in case you'd forgotten.

KATIE. No, I haven't forgotten. (SHE *sets down the case and turns to exit.* HOLMES *moves to cut her off, laying the newspaper on the table.*)

HOLMES. What time is it? (HE *tries to take her wrist.*)

KATIE. Nearly nine. You should go.

HOLMES. That's true then, is it, what you said last night? I turned away from you?

VICTOR. (*Calls.*) Okay.

(HOLMES *glances reflexively at the study door. When* HE *looks back* KATIE *has gone. A moment, then* HOLMES *enters the study.*)

VICTOR. Good morning.

HOLMES. Victor, about last night —

VICTOR. I see is snowed after we went to bed.

HOLMES. Eh? (HE *turns from* VICTOR *to the window behind his desk.*)

VICTOR. I'm going today.

HOLMES. What?

VICTOR. I have to go today as it turns out.

HOLMES. But what about your dissertation?

VICTOR. It's all right.

HOLMES. We haven't talked.

VICTOR. I have to go.

HOLMES. Now look, son, settle down. I'm sorry about last night. I'll get Katie to make you some breakfast and finish it right now.

VICTOR. You have your nine o'clock class.

HOLMES. Where is it?

VICTOR. It's already packed.

HOLMES. This takes me by surprise, Victor. I thought you were staying till Sunday.

VICTOR. I'm sorry but there really doesn't seem much point does there. (HE *picks up his shaving kit.*)

HOLMES. Did I tell you, I've decided to write your introduction?

VICTOR. The thing is I have to stop off in New York. I spoke to my editor this morning. We talked about publishing as soon as I have the opening chapter finished.

HOLMES. You can't do that. You haven't defended it in committee yet. You don't know that it's academically acceptable.

VICTOR. If Wendel does win the Pulitzer, he'll be on every reading list in the country by Fall.

HOLMES. You want me to call this editor for you?

VICTOR. Why?

HOLMES. They're obviously putting pressure on you.

VICTOR. It's all right.

HOLMES. No it's not all right. I understand the temptation of course, but you have your reputation as a scholar to consider. You need guidance. What's his number? What's his name?

VICTOR. This is important to me, sir.

HOLMES. I know that. Of course it is!

VICTOR. There are a lot of factors to be considered.

HOLMES. (*Taking his meaning.*) . . . I see. Yes, I've no

doubt there. (VICTOR *turns to exit.*) Victor, before I write your introduction I want to read that opening chapter. Katie has asked that nothing about her be included. I trust you will respect that wish.

VICTOR. My editor's changed his mind. He doesn't think your writing an introduction will be necessary after all. It was his decision, I'm sorry.

HOLMES. But we didn't talk!

VICTOR. You gave me your opinion of Wendel last night.

HOLMES. Well I was drunk for christ's sake!

VICTOR. In vino veritas.

HOLMES. What did I say?

VICTOR. Let's just say it wasn't exactly complimentary.

HOLMES. And a negative opinion wouldn't fit in with your master plan, is that it? You'd rather just go without a word like he did? Do you want to know what he thought of me? He despised me and everything I stood for, all this! Do you want a story for your book? The night he left he came in here, into my study, and he rearranged my books, all of them. He took every last one and put it somewhere else. I was lost for days. It must have taken him half the night. I probably only missed him by a few minutes the next morning . . .

VICTOR. Sometimes the artist and the scholar are natural enemies.

HOLMES. Is that a line for your book. Are you already turning us into history? (*Pause.*) I'm sorry I can't help you.

VICTOR. You never read it at all did you.

HOLMES. (*With quiet dignity.*) I tried. (*Pause.*) If you—if you should ever meet Wendel, perhaps you could tell him—Never mind. Tell him his mother has stopped drinking.

(VICTOR *goes. For a long moment* HOLMES *does not move, then* HE *slowly, mechanically, begins to prepare his briefcase for class.* HE *looks at the calendar, takes a folder of notes from the file cabinet, and a book from the shelf.* HE *snaps the case shut and picks up his tennis bag and slogs into the living room.* HE *stops, stares out the living room window from a distance, realizes it's pointless to take his tennis things, tosses the tennis bag back in the study, and sets down the briefcase.*)

(HE *picks up the newspaper and opens it. The headline catches his eye.* HE *stops, reads, frowns, and slumps into* KATIE's chair.

KATIE *re-enters to get her coat and scarf from the coat tree.*)


KATIE. You're going to be late. (*No response.*) What's the matter?

HOLMES. The student paper's filled with Ramsey. Look at the headline. He's making this a personal vendetta against me. The 'stagnation of the Department under my Chairpersonship,' my 'lack of with-itness' — and this: he says I ought to be shut off in an ivory tower and only allowed to do unpublished research. (HE *throws the paper down on the table.*)

KATIE. I don't understand. Ramsey said he wasn't going to cause trouble.

HOLMES. No he didn't. I said he said that.

KATIE. Why didn't you tell me?

HOLMES. It doesn't concern you.

KATIE. I'm your wife.

HOLMES. Are you? Well now we're getting somewhere aren't we. The bastard tried to blackmail me. I've put up with a lot here God knows, but by damn I draw the line at that.

KATIE. (SHE *has picked up the paper.*) It says there's going to be a demonstration.

HOLMES. Yes.

KATIE. You're not going are you?

HOLMES. (*Testily.*) I don't know.

KATIE. It would only make matters worse —

HOLMES. (*Snapping.*) I know! (*Suddenly invigorated,* HE *rises and gets his overcoat.*)

KATIE. What are you doing?

HOLMES. I have a class to teach!

KATIE. Holmes —

HOLMES. No! The blood is in the water now and I have a few things to say before I leave here.

KATIE. But you haven't heard from Brandeis yet. You don't know —

HOLMES. There are bridges to be burnt!

KATIE. It might be dangerous.

HOLMES. What do you care? Just so long as they don't come here and torch the house and leave you homeless.

KATIE. You're just asking for trouble.

HOLMES. (*Picking up his briefcase.*) By holding class? On the contrary, experience has shown me that the quickest way to render a group of students harmless is to try to teach them something. It's like whistling at a mad dog, it confuses them. (HE *goes back for his tennis bag.*)

KATIE. What are you doing? You can't play tennis today, haven't you looked outside? It snowed.

HOLMES. You call that snow? Back east, that's where it snows!

KATIE. Holmes, please!

HOLMES. I do not intend to let my routine be upset by

a bunch of lemmings and their pied piper! (HE *goes.*
KATIE *goes quickly to the living room window and
watches anxiously after him.* VICTOR *re-enters.*)

VICTOR. Good morning.

KATIE. (*Turning.*) Oh. Good morning.

VICTOR. I'm leaving momentarily. (HE *goes into the
study, packs the shaving kit in the suitcase which* HE
*then closes.* HE *puts on his suit coat, picks up his bags
and trenchcoat and comes into the living room.* HE *sets
the bags down.*) I owe you an apology, Mrs. Bradford.
I've been rude and I hope you can forgive me. I don't
know what else to say except that I'm sorry. My only de-
fense is my deep feeling for your son's work.

KATIE. I'm the one who should apologize. I've been a
terrible inconvenience to you. I seem to make a mess of
everyone else's life as well as my own.

VICTOR. You say that too easily. I don't think I
believe you. And I don't think you believe it either. You
think it's easier to run yourself down than to admit
you've been cheated. (KATIE *is too surprised by this to
respond.*) I know your whole story. Your husband told
me all about you the first morning I was here. It was
before he knew how you felt. There was no betrayal in-
volved, I couldn't leave without telling you that.

KATIE. I see. Well now that does make me feel rather
foolish.

VICTOR. I don't think you should. What he stressed
most was your self recovery. You must be a very brave
woman. I know something about white-knuckle sobrie-
ty. You have to take it one day at a time, and everything
is a potential temptation, especially emotions.

KATIE. Yes, that's true.

VICTOR. (*Putting on his trenchcoat.*) So the trembling
you mentioned is physical then, from the demon rum?

KATIE. Yes, I suppose that's true.

VICTOR. Is is permanent?

KATIE. . . . Yes.

VICTOR. And what you said last night about paying Wendel to leave, that's true too?

KATIE. (*Alert.*) Why? (VICTOR *does not answer at once.*) Why?

VICTOR. I — I know too much. Mrs. Brandford. Surely you realize there's no way I cannot include —

KATIE. I do not want to become one of the infamous literary mothers of history, even a minor one. I will not be reduced to that.

VICTOR. I can assure you it won't be minor. I think Wendel has a —

KATIE. No!

VICTOR. But without the biographical chapter they won't publish. I've put a year of my life into this. My whole career is riding on it.

KATIE. (*Firmly.*) You are young and you are reportedly very intelligent. You will have many opportunities to distinguish yourself.

VICTOR. (*With equal firmness.*) Mrs. Bradford, believe me I appreciate what you've been through. I appreciate your feelings. I have nothing but respect for you and the struggle you've had to make your peace. But frankly my first loyalty is to Wendel. He deserves our attention and understanding and I will not be thwarted by your guilt. (*His anger rising.*) Okay you screwed up, but you must have screwed up just right because he's out there, Mrs. Bradford, a whole new sensibility, a brand new poetic force holding up the mirror. (*Still angrier.*) I came here in innocence, all right? I didn't plan to find this, I don't know what I expected — a vibrant and loving household? Magic in the air? I wanted to sit at your husband's feet like a disciple, but I think your son means more to me than he does to either one of you. (*Short pause.*) I'm sorry. There's no way for me to make a graceful exit is there. (*Short pause.*) I have to write the truth as I see it.

KATIE. (*Trembling with rage.*) Yes, you write the truth. But you write the whole truth. You describe your research techniques, that's customary isn't it? Describe your duplicity, your lack of decency. Identify yourself! You love Wendel for his sensitivity, is that because you lack all trace of it yourself? You may have come here in innocence but you are not leaving in innocence. Identify yourself! You're a parasite living off my son. You are nothing without my son!

(VICTOR *picks up his bags and goes.*)

## LIGHTS GO TO BLACK

### SCENE SIX

*Late the same afternoon.*

KATIE *is at her table, head down, unconscious. At her elbow* HOLMES' *whiskey bottle and a glass, partly filled. The portfolio case and her coat and scarf are where they were left in the previous scene. The curtains are drawn over the living room window and only a bit of grey winter light filters through.*

*After a moment* HOLMES *enters.* HE *wears his tennis sweats under his overcoat and scarf, and* HE *carries his tennis bag and briefcase. There is a nasty-looking abrasion on the side of his head and a bit of dried blood.* HE *pauses to regard* KATIE — *but does not see the bottle* — *then* HE *crosses slowly into his study.* HE *drops his things;* HE *notices the phone off the hook.*

HOLMES. (*To himself as* HE *replaces it.*) Phone off the hook. Looks like a scene out of Agatha Christie for christ's sake. (KATIE *stirs, comes to.* SHE *glances at her watch, then hears* HOLMES.)

KATIE. Holmes?

HOLMES. (*Still to himself.*) Oops. The corpse just sat up.

KATIE. (*Craning.*) Holmes?

HOLMES. (*Coming to the study doorway.*) How long has the phone been off the hook?

KATIE. (*Rubbing the sleep from her eyes.*) I don't know.

HOLMES. Why?

KATIE. I didn't want to be disturbed.

HOLMES. (*Turning on the light.*) So you finally went the last step to Nirvana, um? Disconnected the phone?

KATIE. (*Seeing his wound.*) What happened?

HOLMES. Tennis accident.

KATIE. Did you fall?

HOLMES. (*Spying the bottle.*) What's this?

KATIE. I'll get a damp towel.

HOLMES. (*Picking up the bottle.*) Katie, what's this all about?

KATIE. I wanted to get drunk.

HOLMES. Is Victor gone?

KATIE. Yes.

HOLMES. God-damnit, Katie!

KATIE. What?

HOLMES. After all these years to let yourself have a relapse?

KATIE. I'm not having a relapse.

HOLMES. No? I walk in and find you sprawled all over your table.

KATIE. I wasn't sprawled, I was asleep.

HOLMES. You're drunk.

KATIE. No I'm not. I had one drink. Half a drink. A sip.

HOLMES. In that order?

KATIE. Just sit down while I get a towel. (SHE *exits. The PHONE RINGS.* HOLMES *answers it quickly.*)

HOLMES. Hello? (*His anticipation changes to anger.*) Yes, this is he and no, I've got nothing more to say. I've made my statement. (HE *slams the phone down and slumps into the swivel chair.*)

KATIE. (*Reappearing with the towel.*) It's those contacts, you're still not used to them. (SHE *wipes the wound.*) It's all dried. How long ago did this happen?

HOLMES. Awhile.

KATIE. Why didn't you go to the infirmary?

HOLMES. When I have a perfectly good nurse at home? (*The PHONE RINGS again.* HOLMES *snatches it up.*)

HOLMES. Yes? (*Sharply.*) I told you I have nothing more to say! (HE *hangs up.*)

KATIE. What was that? Holmes, who was that?

HOLMES. The yellow press.

KATIE. What?

HOLMES. A reporter.

KATIE. Why? Holmes, what happened?

HOLMES. (*Grinning in spite of himself; as if announcing a triumph.*) Katie, this has been quite a day.

KATIE. Was there a demonstration?

HOLMES. Just like the paper ordered. I tried to ignore it, I did, but they made that impossible so I let 'em have it.

KATIE. Have what?

HOLMES. Both barrels, right between the eyes. Twenty-five years off my chest.

KATIE. What did you say?

HOLMES. (HE *rises to remove his hat and scarf and to move into the living room where* HE *drops them on the furniture.*) I began my reminding them what a university was for and jesus did that set them off. Some enterprising radical made a tape recording of my whole tirade and played it over a speaker system in the South Oval. Holmes Bradford: Instant Villain. By the time I met with my afternoon seminar there was a crowd of dozens — hundreds if you count the curious — trampling the bushes outside the windows, chanting their heads off. Someone even threw a rock.

KATIE. Is that — ? (SHE *indicates the wound.*)

HOLMES. Yes. My seminar fled, which confirmed something I've always suspected about graduate students, but I continued to discuss death and circumference in Emily Dickinson till the end of the hour.

KATIE. To an empty room?

HOLMES. I told you I wasn't going to let them disrupt my routine didn't I.

KATIE. Did that rock give you a concussion?

HOLMES. And then it was off to the tennis courts!

KATIE. In the snow?

HOLMES. Yes!

KATIE. What about the students?

HOLMES. They came with me. I ignored them which only made them madder. They surrounded the courts and shook the cyclone fence in a fury, while I calmly swept the snow off my court.

KATIE. And then?

HOLMES. I changed into my tennis things.

KATIE. What do you mean?

HOLMES. I altered my external appearance.

KATIE. How?

HOLMES. I took off my clothes.

KATIE. Under your coat?

HOLMES. Not on your life.

KATIE. Holmes —

HOLMES. I stripped! Right there on the tennis court in

front of all of them. Right down to mother nature! There was no more heckling after that. I know what you mean by silence now, hon.

KATIE. And there were reporters there?

HOLMES. Reporters? There was a television crew! Katie, I've finally made it! I've been dragged kicking and screaming into the Twentieth Century. I'm going to be on television!

KATIE. Television!

HOLMES. Waving my tallywacker right in the cameraman's face!

KATIE. No!

HOLMES. Well doesn't the public have a right to know? It's the rare days of anarchy all over again, isn't it, Kate? It's just like old times when we did everything with verse and hunger? (*Grinning broadly with a new thought.*) This will make it a little uncomfortable for you if you stay here, eh? Think of the gossip that will attach itself to the recluse wife of an exhibitionist professor of departed memory.

KATIE. Is that why you did it?

HOLMES. Well I don't know, maybe it was. How about that?

KATIE. What will Brandeis say?

HOLMES. I don't know . . . I haven't thought about that. (HE *hasn't. His bravado falters.*) That's the first rule of verse and hunger isn't it? Do as the spirit moves you and don't count the cost?

KATIE. Did you really take everything off?

HOLMES. Yes, I'm afraid I did . . . After I spoke my piece this morning I thought that would be it, but the students kept dogging me, their numbers kept growing, and the next thing I knew there I was on the tennis courts, surrounded. It was like waking from a dream and discovering reality was the nightmare. So I thought, okay, this is what it all comes down to. Ramsey is forgotten, my tirade is forgotten, all my years here — it all comes down to this moment: they are waiting for me to admit that I can't play tennis by myself on a court covered with snow.

KATIE. What did you do? I mean, if you were alone?

HOLMES. I practised my serve. (HE *smiles briefly in triumph, then:*) I can explain it to Brandeis can't I? They'll understand won't they?

KATIE. (*Taking his hands.*) Bravo. You did the absolutely correct and proper thing, and don't spoil it with second thoughts. Of course anyone can have a breakdown —

HOLMES. It wasn't a breakdown!

KATIE. I'm teasing.

HOLMES. (*Surprised.*) Oh. (HE *glances at her watch and rises uneasily.*) It's after four, why haven't they called?

KATIE. The phone was off the hook.

HOLMES. Well they could've called the office.

KATIE. I think you need to lie down.

HOLMES. I can't. The cot smells of hairspray. (*At this reference to* VICTOR, KATIE *turns to busy herself collecting some sheafs of drawings at the side table and putting them into a cardboard folder. But* SHE *does not appear distressed.*) I'm sorry about Victor.

KATIE. That's past now, we can forget it.

HOLMES. (*Shifting uneasily.*) Well I have a confession to make. It seems I told him all about you.

KATIE. (*Chiding gently.*) Oh? Seems?

HOLMES. I gave him a whole case history. I had no idea you were going to come so — unglued . . . You're not upset?

KATIE. No.

HOLMES. (*With some edge.*) That's odd.

KATIE. At least Wendel will find out that I'm better.

HOLMES. He won't read Victor's book. He wouldn't

soil his hands with anything written by an academic.

KATIE. I think he will. He's much too conceited not to. (*Pause.*) Is his poetry really that good?

HOLMES. No. Not yet. But if he sticks to it . . . If I could just talk to him, point out a few things . . . The prick.

KATIE. No . . . I think we raised an orphan, you and I. Victor did say one thing: we must have screwed up in just the right way because he *is* out there, a whole new sensibility. And now maybe some day — I just hope he's happy . . .

HOLMES. Katie, I can't stay on here, not after today. Even if Brandeis says no I'll have to go. Somewhere . . . I can't go without you. I need you.

KATIE. You haven't been happy with me, Holmes. Not for a very long time.

HOLMES. If you stay here alone you'll become a recluse, I know you. And I couldn't bear that. I'll leave you alone. We don't have to talk. I won't look at you. "Sole Kate" — ?

KATIE. This morning, after Victor left, I felt so awful I tried to take a drink. But I couldn't, I didn't want it. I think it's finally over. I don't have to be afraid of that any more.

HOLMES. There, you see? Good for you, Katie —

KATIE. But then the thing I'd been so frightened of happened: the past came back. The distant past, the years before everything went haywire. I remembered winning that art scholarship to Paris. I remembered how I thought I saw my whole life before me. I was going to astonish the world — or at least other artists. But then I realized that the things I remembered most vividly had nothing to do with competition and fame. I barely remembered the art school at all, but I could see so clearly the little room I had all to myself with its lace curtains so delicate they could always find a breeze. I remembered being happiest on the boat going over because for nine whole days I was alone for the first time in my life, free of the earth. And the privacy of not knowing the language! I remembered the pressure of my brush on the canvas, as delicate as the breeze in the curtains, as delicate as the sound of your voice when you read. Those were the things I loved the most, and nothing else has ever had to matter. You were right last night when you said I wanted to be left alone, but the thought of that terrifies me now.

HOLMES. Then you'll stay with me?

KATIE. Someone has to keep you from taking off your clothes in public. (SHE *picks up her coat.*)

HOLMES. Katie—do you know why I never replaced my watch after it broke? Because it's the one excuse I have to touch you.

KATIE. But you must let me come as I am.

HOLMES. I will, I do. It's all forgotten. I'll let the past go, I swear. We'll live in the present, we'll live for the future, and if someday you do surprise me—

KATIE. (*Quickly, firmly.*) No. You must not worry about me.

HOLMES. But I do, Katie—

KATIE. You mustn't, I can't bear it, please.

HOLMES. —because I love you.

KATIE. (SHE *embraces him with her whole being.*) Please. (*After a long moment,* SHE *disengages and slips into her coat.*)

HOLMES. Where are you going?

KATIE. The Art Barn.

HOLMES. Now?

KATIE. It's Friday. I have my class to teach.

HOLMES. You're going to make me wait for the phone call alone?

KATIE. Call me the minute you hear. (SHE *picks up*

*the folder and goes.* HOLMES *rubs his hands on his sweat pants nervously.* HE *goes into the study.* HE *hovers over the phone and finally snatches the receiver off the hook and puts it in the top desk drawer. Then* HE *turns and searches the shelves.* HE *takes down a book and goes back into the living room.* HE *stops by* KATIE'S *table and looks at the painting on the wall.*)

HOLMES. (*Quoting from memory "Music I Heard With You", by Conrad Aiken.*)
"Music I heard with you was more than music
And bread I broke with you was more than bread."
( HE *looks at the table, touching it lightly.*)
"Your hands have touched this table and this silver
And I have seen your fingers hold this glass.
These things do not remember you, beloved,
And yet your touch upon them shall not pass."

( *As the LIGHTS begin to fade* HE *crosses to the window, draws back the curtain, and sits on the window seat with the book in his lap to await* KATIE'S *return.*)

LIGHTS GO TO BLACK.

END OF PLAY.

## PROPERTY PLOT:

Brought on by actors:
Transfer slip (Stoddard)
Straw bag with weeds, dried grasses, leaves (Katie)
Suitcase (packed by wardrobe) (Victor)
   Also containing: Shaving kit
Attache case, containing:
   Copy of dissertation (about 200 pages, bound)
   Steno notebook
   Pencils and pens
   Cassette tape recorder (Victor)
Student newspaper w/ rubber band (Holmes)
Two cups and saucers with cream and coffee (Katie)
Shoebox with snapshots (Victor)
Facecloth (Katie)
Tray, containing:
   Water pitcher
   Water glass
   Two cups and saucers w/ coffee
   Teaspoons
   Creamer w/ cream (Katie)
Styrofoam cup w/ a small amount of coffee (Ramsey)
Six or eight pieces of mail (Katie)
Handkerchief (Holmes)
Lunch tray w/ sandwich on plate, glass of juice
(Katie)

Onstage; living room:
   Round table: Poster
   Tray w/ inks
   Pens
   Drawing pad

Scratch paper
Three calligraphy books
Water glass
Loose ink
Correction fluid
Side table: Sewing box, w/thread and needle
Cardboard file (about 10″ × 15″) w/ tie string
Sheaf of children's drawings
Vase w/ weeds, dried grasses, etc.
Window seat: Large portfolio case
Art books

Onstage, study:
Tray, w/ water pitcher, glass
Thermometer (hanging near door)
Several manilla folders w/ lecture notes (in file
  cabinet)
Burger King bag (I iii)
Bourbon bottle (open) behind books in bookcase
Two glasses, with bourbon bottle
Alarm, clock, on desk
Space heater, on floor near desk
Pillow, on reading chair
Blanket, on cot
Phone book (small, containing white and yellow
  pages, for a town of perhaps 50,000) on floor
Thesis (about 200 pages, in mailing envelope) under
  magazines and/or books on top of filing cabinet
Old briefcase (with folder containing typed letter and
  contact lens case) on floor near desk
Six books, in various bookshelves
Tennis bag, with racket, on floor

On the desk:
Kleenex box, with kleenex
Rubber bands

Exam books (blue books)
Mint bowl, with mints
Notepad
Pens, pencils

## COSTUME PLOT:

HOLMES:

Scene: 1 Thermal nightshift
Old, dun colored flannel bathrobe
Slippers

2 Old tweed jacket       Old overcoat
Plaid shirt            Hat
Solid-colored tie (either straight tie or bow)
Solid-colored slacks (wool or corduroy)

3 Old sweater (cardigan or pullover)
Shirt (different from I-ii)

4 Old overcoat
For the rest, more or less the same as I-ii.

5 A dark, three-piece suit slightly out of date

6 Grey sweat pants
Green t-shirt or turtleneck
Maroon sweater with a few holes
Tennis shoes
Scarf

KATIE:

Scene: 1 Flannel nightgown
Plain blue corduroy housecoat
Slippers

2 The same, later change to:
Simple skirt, blouse, sweater (cardigan), flats.

3 Plain overcoat
Pullover sweater
Functional boots (perhaps galloshes)

4 Same as 1

5 Skirt and blouse

6 Same as 5.

94

VICTOR:

Scene: 1  Suit, Continental style (tailored) of grey wool
            White shirt
            Tie
            New trenchcoat, beige, with epaulets
            Polished shoes
        2  Fashionable slacks, well pressed
            Dress shirt, long-sleeved
            (Add) V-neck sweater
        3  Same slacks as 2
            Same suit coat as 1
            Different dress shirt
            Same sweater as 2
        4  Same as 1
        5  Same as 4

STODDARD OATES:

Scene: 2  Dark red wind-breaker
            Madras shirt
            Blue jeans

RAMSEY:

Scene: 3  Tight, pre-faded blue jeans
            Tailored corduroy jacket with elbow patches
            Powder blue work shirt
            Cowboy boots
            Suede jacket with sheepskin lining
            Cowboy hat (optional)

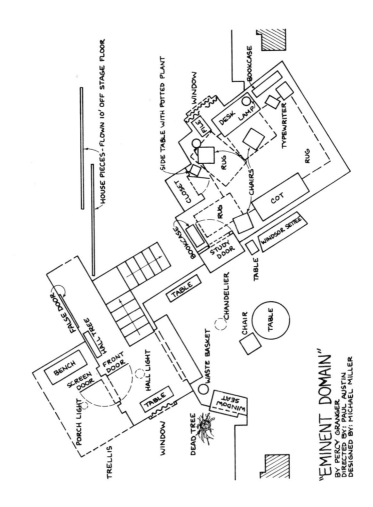

"EMINENT DOMAIN"
BY PERCY GRANGER.
DIRECTED BY: PAUL AUSTIN
DESIGNED BY: MICHAEL MILLER

96